SWORD AND PEN

Other Poetry Titles by AUP

AGAINST LEVIATHAN
Norman Kreitman

TOUCHING ROCK
Norman Kreitman

THE LOW ROAD HAME
Donald Gordon

POEMS OF THE SCOTTISH HILLS
an anthology
Hamish Brown

SPEAK TO THE HILLS
an anthology of twentieth century British and Irish mountain poetry
Hamish Brown and Martyn Berry

TIME GENTLEMEN
Hamish Brown

A RESURRECTION OF A KIND
Christopher Rush

PERSPECTIVES
George Bruce

SWORD
AND
PEN

POEMS OF 1915 FROM DUNDEE AND TAYSIDE

edited by

HILDA D SPEAR AND BRUCE PANDRICH

ABERDEEN UNIVERSITY PRESS

Member of Maxwell Macmillan Pergamon Publishing Corporation

First published 1989
Aberdeen University Press
© Introduction and Selection Hilda D Spear and Bruce Pandrich 1989

The publisher acknowledges subsidy from the Scottish Arts Council towards
publication of this volume.

British Library Cataloguing in Publication Data

Sword and pen: poems of 1915 from Dundee and Tayside.
1. Poetry in English. Scottish writers. 1900–1945.
Special subjects. World War I. Anthologies
I. Spear, Hilda D (Hilda Doris), *1926*— II. Pandrich,
Bruce
821'.912'080358

ISBN 0 08 037960 5

PRINTED IN GREAT BRITAIN
THE UNIVERSTY PRESS
ABERDEEN

In memory of those who died at Loos
25 September–13 October 1915

CONTENTS

PREFACE

The poems in this book have been collected together in memory of the Scottish soldiers who died in battle during the black year of 1915, particularly the men of the 4th Black Watch who were killed at Loos. It is intended also as a tribute to the wounded and bereaved of that time. The poems have been gleaned from the local newspapers of 1915; most of them were written by poets from Dundee and the surrounding area or by poets connected with Scottish Regiments or with the Battle of Loos. A small percentage, though published locally, originate elsewhere but are relevant to the general theme of the book. If anyone reading the poems has memories or, indeed, information of any kind connected with either the poems or their authors we should be very grateful if they will get in touch with us at the university.

Hilda D Spear
Bruce Pandrich

ACKNOWLEDGEMENTS

The editors gratefully acknowledge assistance given by Dundee University Library, the Local History Department of the Central Library of Dundee and the Black Watch Museum in Perth. Thanks are also due to Mr D W Longair whose wide knowledge of the military matters of the period has been generously shared with us.

We should also like to acknowledge the kindness of relatives of poets who have allowed us to publish poems. If we have inadvertently published without permission any poems which appear to be in copyright, we apologise and should be grateful if the copyright owner would get in touch with us.

We also offer our thanks to those people from Dundee and the Tayside Region in particular, and from the east of Scotland in general, who have given us assistance in various ways.

INTRODUCTION

Every year on 25 September the light on the Law War Memorial in Dundee shines out to commemorate the dead of the Battle of Loos. The Battle has been described variously as 'Dundee's Flodden' or 'Dundee's Verdun', but, more exactly and never to be forgotten, it is 'Dundee's Loos', a name imprinted on the heart of almost every family living in Dundee in 1915.

When war broke out on 4 August 1914 the territorials of the 4th Battalion of the Black Watch were immediately mobilised. The Battalion was drawn almost exclusively from Dundee, from the City's 'Three Js'—the jute mills, the jam factories and the journalistic enterprises of the Thomson-Leng empire. It represented, as the official history of the Black Watch suggests, 'a Scottish city at war' and for the people of Dundee the fluctuating fortunes of the 4th Battalion were the fluctuating fortunes of war. Their first wartime duty was that of coastal defence; two companies were sent to guard the Tay Bridge, two to protect Broughty Ferry from the enemy and three companies were stationed in Dundee itself to guard the city's water supply, the docks and the submarine dry dock. In retrospect the precautions appear to be futile and simplistic; their greatest value was perhaps psychological, in that they encouraged a sense of community: the men of Dundee were joined together in an act of solidarity to protect their own city and the non-combatant citizens were comforted and felt safe because their own menfolk were defending them. Simultaneously, however, the men were being prepared for war and were being given intensive training, as well as practice in musketry at Buddon.

The 4th Battalion, like many other battalions of the First World War—the '"Pals" Battalions'—comprised family groups, fathers and sons, brothers, uncles, cousins and formed an intimately familiar unit, coming from a close-knit community. They were proud and eager to serve their country and looked forward with enthusiasm to the promise of a more active role than that of home defence. Their opportunity came on 23 February 1915 when the Battalion received orders to move to France. The local papers expressed the feelings of the city:

> If Dundee has taken leave of her soldier sons with regret it is with pride as well; for the selection of the Battalion to form a part of the Territorial Forces on foreign service is no small honour to the city

claimed *The Dundee Advertiser* on 24 February 1915 and *The Courier and Argus* for the same day reported that

> the 4th (Service) Battalion of The Black Watch—Dundee's Own—left the city yesterday evening and dense crowds gave them a stirring send-off . . . It was a well-set-up gritty battalion upon which the citizens of Dundee last night showered thunderous cheers as they marched from Dudhope Castle to the West Station.

It was an excitement and enthusiasm replicated all over the country; the young men of Dundee, like the other young men of Britain, were looking for honour and glory, even for the chance of dying as heroes. Death itself seemed to hold no terror for them. They sang on their way to the station, the pipe bands played and the onlookers shouted and cheered. Had the dense crowds of that evening been told that in seven months their joy would be turned to mourning they would not have comprehended it.

It is not difficult to account for the euphoria of that time; schoolboys were fed on romantic tales of courage and adventure and lived vicariously in the noble exploits of others; the war gave them a chance to escape from their own mundane lives into the very stories that had excited them. 'Life' commented Philip Gibbs in *Now It Can Be Told*, 'had been rather dull in office and factory and on the farm'. Consequently, recruiting offices throughout the country were besieged by would-be soldiers and excitement was at fever-pitch. The territorials of the 4th Black Watch felt themselves especially privileged to be sent to France to fight beside the regular troops. On the eve of their departure, their commanding officer, Colonel Harry Walker, addressed the battalion in stirring words:

> The chance has come for you to show in the field those high qualities which have always made the 4th Battalion Black Watch a Territorial Battalion with which it is an honour to be associated. Men, you belong to a great Regiment, one whose battalions of the line have gathered glory and reaped fame in every quarter of the globe and I trust when you proceed on active service . . . you will remember that tradition and do your best to garner fresh laurels for the Black Watch.

No mention was made of the possibility of death or worse, for the men were looking for glory and fame, the chance to experience life to the full. Despite the killed and wounded of the early months of the war the romantic myth of heroism died hard; Julian Grenfell, who had been in France since October 1914, described his regiment as they moved up to the Front Line at Ypres just about the time that the 4th were embarking for France: 'You should have seen our men setting out from here for the trenches—absolutely radiant with excitement and joy to be getting back to the fight'. He wrote his well-known poem 'Into Battle' after being engaged in the Second Battle of Ypres:

> The naked earth is warm with Spring,
>   And with green grass and bursting trees
> Leans to the sun's gaze glorying,
>   And quivers in the sunny breeze;
> And Life is Colour and Warmth and Light,
>   And a striving evermore for these;
> And he is dead who will not fight,
>   And who dies fighting has increase.

Less than a month later Grenfell was dead but the sentiments of 'Into Battle' were universally embraced; most of Dundee's soldiers were caught up in the general excitement that saw their contribution to the war not as an obligation but as an opportunity.

The territorials of the 4th Black Watch joined their regular comrades of the 1st and 2nd Battalions in France and by the end of May 1915 the 5th, 6th, 7th, 8th and 9th Battalions also arrived there. The men of the 5th Battalion came mainly from Angus, in particular from Forfar and the fishing villages along the coast, Arbroath, Montrose and Broughty Ferry; the 6th Battalion was from Perthshire and the 7th from the mining towns of Fife. In their book on *The Black Watch* Eric and Andro Linklater comment with reference to the Battle of Loos that not since Culloden had so many Scottish soldiers been in the field at the same time. Certainly during 1914 and 1915 there was a massive Scottish presence in France and the 'In Memoriam' columns of the national papers bear witness to the fact that the men of many Scots regiments were fighting and dying to defend their country.

The 4th Battalion arrived in France on the morning of 26 February 1915; during the ensuing months they were engaged in action at Neuve Chapelle and at Festubert and sustained considerable losses; at the end of May, however, they were withdrawn from the Front and did not engage in any serious action again until the Battle of Loos began on 25 September. It was one of the most wasteful and mismanaged battles in a war that was notable for wasteful and mismanaged battles. In his autobiography *The Pageant of the Years*, Philip Gibbs succinctly describes the catalogue of disasters that occurred:

The Battle of Loos was a ghastly failure after the first smash through. The reserves—the two fresh divisions—were held too far back and came up too late. When they did arrive they were unprovided with maps, knew nothing about the ground, and made an awful mess of things, through no fault of their own. Our forward line, very thin now, received no support at the right time and was in no strength to resist enemy counterattacks. At the beginning of the battle a disaster occurred, because the gas we were using was blown back on to the Black Watch by a veering wind.

The 4th Battalion suffered very heavy losses; over half of the men and twenty of the twenty-one officers were killed or wounded; Colonel Walker, whose brave words had inspired the battalion as they left Dundee, was among the dead. After the battle the 4th Battalion was so reduced that it was amalgamated with the 5th Battalion and the 'city at war' became a more diffuse entity.

Over seventy years later the Battle of Loos is remembered in Dundee with grief and disbelief. It was a battle that left almost every family in the city in mourning. Yet, despite the shock and horror, romance did not die; the headlines in local newspapers perpetuated the myth of glory: 'Fought Like Tigers', they ran, 'Famous Victory', 'Black Watch Gallantry', 'Victory Won in the Rain'. Somehow, courage and ferocity in the battle were interpreted as success: 'There was no holding our men back', wrote one Black Watch soldier in a letter published in *The Courier and Argus* for 7 October 1915, '. . . our officers led in great style . . . The general said we had fought like tigers and thanked us for all the work we had done.' In the same paper, on 30 September, Colonel Walker's death had been reported in terms consonant with his brave speech to his men on the eve of embarkation:

> Colonel Walker did not make the supreme sacrifice in vain . . . With many others he fell on the field of glory, and his death should be an incentive to every young eligible man to do his duty for King and Country.

Despite the terrible losses the City and its environs had sustained there was no general condemnation of the war; criticism there certainly was but bitterness and disillusion were not dominant. Mr J B Taylor, President of the Dundee Chamber of Commerce at the time addressed the Chamber in words that must have reflected the mood of the city: 'I need scarcely say that any meeting in our city at present must be a sad one, for we are living under the shadow of perhaps the blackest cloud that we have ever experienced . . .' Much of the traditional language of sacrifice and glory was, nevertheless, used to describe the battle. The Battalion medical officer told *The Dundee Advertiser* in an interview published on 23 October that the 'deeds of the 4th Black Watch on 25th September may have been equalled, but they have never been excelled. The bravery and gallantry of the officers and men were an example to all . . .' Another nine months of hardship and misery were to pass before the opening of the Battle of the Somme heralded the failure of hope, the growth of pessimism and the beginning of the war of attrition.

Throughout the whole of the war period local and national newspapers published verse from both the war and home fronts. In times of stress many people turn to poetry, some as readers and many more as writers. The poems in this book were published in *The Dundee Advertiser* and *The People's Journal* during 1915. They cover the period from the arrival of the 4th Black Watch in France to its near-destruction and amalgamation with the 5th after the Battle of Loos. They may be seen as poems that comforted or inspired the people of Dundee before, during and after the losses of that terrible battle. It is in no way surprising that most of them are romantic, glorifying courage and heroism, exulting in the exploits of particular heroic figures, delighting in regimental fame and ignoring the realities of battle, the woundings and the deaths. Even Loos with its terrible carnage did not destroy the spirit of the 'Tommies' and the 'Jocks'. The poems of Dundee and the east of Scotland followed the pattern of the poetry of the day. It was not until the anti-war poems of Siegfried Sassoon, Wilfred Owen and others, written after the Battle of the Somme in mid 1916, showed war in its true colours, that lesser poets found themselves able to write realistically about its horrors.

What is perhaps most striking about the verse being produced during the war is, first, that many ordinary men and women were turning to poetry to express their deepest and most heartfelt emotions and secondly, that such verse was published regularly in the newspapers and read by thousands of people who would not normally think of themselves as lovers of poetry. In some ways such popular verse may be seen as contributing to an understanding and interpretation of the war; particularly that published in local papers frequently dealt with matters of deep moment to the readers. So, in the Dundee papers, much of the verse referred to the battle exploits of the Black Watch and often to men well-known in the area who had gone to France with the 4th. It shows a direct and occasionally subtle response to the events of the day and was perhaps partly responsible for directing and shaping the reactions of the civilian population.

Some of the poems included in this book were written by serving men; many were written by people left at home. Whilst it is not always easy to distinguish between soldiers' poetry and that of civilians, one can say that, by and large, the two points of view differ: the verse written by serving soldiers reflects aspects of life at the Front, whilst the civilian verse focuses on the reactions of those left at home. Both viewpoints are frequently romantic, seeing life at the Front as fraught with danger but, nevertheless, full of opportunities for glory and heroism or, alternatively, showing how proud were wives, mothers and sweethearts to see their men in uniform and how gladly they gave them to die for their country. Both groups seemed to be trying to convince themselves and others that war was still glorious and thus to find comfort in bereavement. Yet some of the verse from soldiers begins to approach realistic thought after they have been in battle and seen the terrible human suffering:

> Soldier, soldier, charging on the foe,
> With your comrade's dying cry to urge you as you go.
> Soldier, soldier, stilly lying dead,
> With a dum-dum bullet through your dunderhead.
> (Joseph Lee, 'The Green Grass')

Such lines are in stark contrast with the poem published in *The Dundee Advertiser* in the middle of the Battle of Loos, which exhorted mothers to send their sons to war:

> Oh Mothers! The empire needeth,
> The sons ye bravely bore.
> Oh, Mothers! The Empire calleth
> Your sons to end the War.
> (G M S, 'Mothers')

The dead soldier with a dum-dum bullet through his head appears to have little connection with the sons who are being sent to 'end the War' and the bravery has been curiously attributed to the mothers rather than to their soldier sons.

The emotional range of the poems is, in fact, greater than the foregoing quotations would imply, though none of them achieves the tragic proportions of the work of the realist poets of the later war years. Most of what was written, however, was simple and unadventurous in both form and style but such simplicity achieved a universality that more sophisticated poetry could not. Most of the poems were written in four- or eight-line stanzas; most of them rhymed and used simple rhyme schemes; most employed romantic 'poetic' diction; some were imitations or parodies of well-known poems; some were written to be sung to popular tunes; some responded to verse printed in the same paper earlier; some were personal tributes to soldiers who had performed 'heroic' deeds; some were responses to an event of topical interest; some were laudatory; some were critical. Many dealt with issues of contemporary significance, picking up and commenting on moral and idealistic questions which were popular subjects of discussion. Probably all were therapeutic, either for the writers or for the readers.

In printing such poems the local newspapers were falling back on the old tradition which enshrined great events in ballads. The oral tradition of the ballads was translated into a modern medium but the purpose served was in many ways very similar—it involved the whole community in the exploits performed on their behalf. If the tone and language of the poems often seem inappropriate to their subjects it is because the writers had been conditioned to respond in particular ways. Nothing in their experience had prepared them to believe that war was anything but glorious, that death in battle could be painful, lingering and horrific, that soldiers might suffer terrible psychological damage as they killed and plundered, offending against the Commandments which they had been brought up to believe were sacrosanct. Equally, nothing in the educational and literary experience of most men and women had encouraged them to employ a poetic style at odds with tradition in order to write of events and feelings at odds with the traditional values of honour, decency and respect for life.

The verses in this book, therefore, will be seen as traditional, often sentimental expressions of popular thought. Their weakness lies in the fact that they are not original, polished poems of enduring quality. Their strength lies in their reflection of the ideas and emotions which moved the men and women of Dundee and its environs in one of the darkest years of their history; they show an intense commitment to fighting the war and an unbounded admiration for courage and heroism; at the same time, some of them attempt to confront the moral issues that war involved them in and at least a number of the combatant poets hint at a developing attitude to war which does not take for granted the slaughter of millions of victims to achieve an uncertain end.

Many poems were published anonymously or the writer was identified simply by initials or by a pseudonym. Yet there are poets whose names appear again and again. Foremost and probably the best of these is the Dundee artist and journalist, Joseph Lee who, despite being nearly forty at the time, joined the territorials soon after the outbreak of war, went to France with the 4th Black Watch, fought in and survived the Battle of Loos and in 1917 was captured in the fighting around Cambrai and spent the rest of the war in a prison camp. The verse he regularly sent back to *The Dundee Advertiser* caught the mood of the time and was immensely popular; yet he was one of the writers who did not merely glorify war but attempted to put it in some kind of perspective, often forcing his readers to ponder on the implications of battle:

> Every bullet has its billet,
> Many bullets more than one:
> God! Perhaps I killed a mother
> When I killed a mother's son.
> ('The Bullet')

The simplicity and force of the last two lines is a precursor of the poetry of the war realists and shows an intellectual grasp of the problems of war as they affected the ordinary soldier. The fact that he neither strove for cunning stylistic effects nor employed traditionally poetic language but, rather, preferred to write in a style akin to that of the old Scottish ballads enhanced the impact of his poetry. Yet the very simplicity of this quatrain serves to hide its technical skill with the repetition of 'bullet . . . bullets . . . killed a mother . . . killed a mother's son' and with the internal chiming on 'bullet' and 'billet'.

Few of the other poets show this kind of technical skill or, indeed, deal with the moral and psychological worries (as distinct from the physical) that war presents. The early, pacifist poem by Ruth Comfort Mitchell is, however, worth looking at for its deliberate use of the light-hearted rythms of the 'death or glory' poetry:

> . . . . They were fine, new flags that swung a flying there,
> Oh, the pretty girls he glimpsed a-crying there,
> Pelting him with pinks and with roses—
> Billy, the Soldier Boy.

But the 'knightly joke of it' soon fades in the face of reality and the poem ends with the horror of Billy's death on the battlefield and a condemnation of the 'braggart attitudes' and 'tinsel platitudes' which have served to encourage war; the use throughout the poem of the same light-hearted rhythm which was used to relate Billy's proud and mindless approach to battle underlines the irony of war's reality. What is perhaps surprising is not that such a poem should have been written in the early days of the war but that it should have been published.

The poetry of the period, however, displays many varying attitudes and blatant contradictions, reflecting the confused reactions to events as they occurred. In some way poetry came into its own. Hundreds of poems were published in the local papers; though most of them were by local writers, some were reprinted from other papers and some were well-known poems published in order to offer comfort to the sorrowing or bereaved. The healing effect of such poems is difficult to calculate but it seems unlikely that we can understand fully the impact of the First World War without taking into consideration what was written, read and accepted by the masses as a natural expression of what they had to endure.

This book is principally concerned with the people of Dundee and its environs during the 'black year' of 1915 and the Battle of Loos and the poems it contains are often localised and immediate. We should like to end this Introduction, therefore, with a poem of more universal implications, yet one that was written by a young Aberdeen-born poet who, though he left his native-land at the age of five, nevertheless fought and died with his fellow-countrymen at Loos. Charles Hamilton Sorley, a Captain in the 7th Suffolks, was killed by a sniper's bullet on 13 October 1915, when he was just over twenty years old; he left as his memorial one of the most powerful poems of the early war period:

> When you see millions of the mouthless dead
> Across your dreams in pale battalions go,
> Say not soft things as other men have said,
> That you'll remember, For you need not so.
> Give them not praise. For, deaf, how should they know
> It is not curses heaped on each gashed head?
> Nor tears. Their blind eyes see not your tears flow.
> Nor honour. It is easy to be dead.
> Say only this, "They are dead.' Then add thereto,
> 'Yet many a better one has died before.'
> Then, scanning all the o'ercrowded mass, should you
> Perceive one face that you loved heretofore
> It is a spook. None wears the face you knew.
> Great death has made all his for evermore.

Hilda D Spear
Bruce Pandrich
Dundee University
July 1989

xxi

Anon

THE OFFICER'S FUNERAL

Hark to the shrill trumpet calling,
   It pierceth the soft summer air;
Tears from each comrade are falling,
   The widow and orphan are there.

The bayonets earthward are turning,
   The drums' muffled breath rolls around;
But he hears not the voice of their mourning,
   Nor wakes to the bugle sound.

Sleep, soldier, though many regret thee
   Who stand by the cold bier today,
Soon, soon will the kindest forget thee,
   And thy name from the earth pass away.

The man thou didst love as a brother,
   A friend in thy room shall have gained;
The dog shall keep watch for another,
   And thy steed by a stranger be reigned.

The hearts that now mourn for thee sadly
   Soon joyous as ever shall be;
Your bright orphan boy may laugh gladly
   As he sits on some kind comrade's knee.

There is one who will still pay the duty
   Of tears to the true and the brave,
As when first in the bloom of her beauty
   She wept o'er her soldier's grave.

The People's Journal, 23 January 1915

Anon

RECRUITING SONG

Why suld we heed, callants, why suld we heed
The folk across the Channel, their colour or their need?
Because we hate the tyrant, where'er his blow may fa',
In Scotland or in Belgium! Because we're brithers a'!

Why maun we 'list, callants, why maun we 'list?
Oor hames are bien and kindly, and sairly we'll be missed.
Because brave mates are calling, because the 'oor has struck
To join them in the trenches, and share the sodger's luck!

Why need we fecht, callants, why face the foe?
Because he seeks to daunt us, and thinks to lay us low:
Because his shells are crushin' amang oor verra doors;
Because oor country calls us to haud him off oor shores!

Wha'd bide at hame, callants, wha'd bide at hame?
To sit in idle comfort, or play the witless game?
Oor sires, when Honour beckoned, bore aye the battle's brunt;
Shall Scotsmen sell their birthricht? Nay! Let us to the front!

*The Dundee Advertiser,*12 February 1915

Anon

THE COMFORTER

Silent in the house I sit
In the fire-light and knit;
At my ball of soft grey wool
Two grey kittens gently pull—
Pulling back my thoughts as well
From that distant red-rimmed hell,
And hot tears the stitches blur
As I knit a comforter.

'Comforter' they call it—yes,
Such it is for my distress,
For it gives my restless hands
Blessed work. God understands
How we women yearn to be
Doing something ceaselessly—
Anything but just to wait
Idly for a clicking gate!

So I knit—this long grey thing
Which some fearless lad will fling
Round him in the icy blast,
With the shrapnel whistling past;
'Comforter' it may be then,
Like a mother's touch again,
And at last, not grey, but red
Be a pillow for the dead.

The Dundee Advertiser, 3 March 1915

Anon

TRANSFORMATION

I throw my youthful garments with the rest,
  With flowers, and calm, and day of mirthful play,
My heart is leaping high within my breast;
  I shut the door on youth and turn away.

And now a naked sword lies in my hand,
  And I am filled with fierce and sudden joy.
I stand erect and wait the hour's command,
  I am a man, I am no more a boy.

The Dundee Advertiser, 13 March 1915

Anon

THE PATRIOTIC WORKMAN

Breathes there a man with soul so dead
Who never to himself hath said,
This is my own, my native land,
Upon her soil shall no foe stand,
While to me the breath from heaven,
Strength to work and fight are given,
I'll dig the coal and iron ore,
I'll feed the blast, the metal pour,
I'll forge the steel and form the shell,
I'll turn the wood, weave cloth as well;
No soldier countryman of mine
Shall lack munitions in the line,
Nor stinted be of food or wear,
My strength and time with him I'll share;

If such there breathe, go, mark him well;
In solemn tones the verdict tell,
Disgrace be his if in this hour
A selfish thought should gain the power,
And he should strike, or shirk, or whine,
While warworn brothers bleed and pine,
He still may live, forfeit renown,
And, doubly dying, shall go down
To the vile dust, from whence he sprung,
Unwept, unhonoured, and unsung.

The People's Journal, 24 April 1915

Anon

AN APPEAL

When we read the magnificent story
    Of all that our heroes achieve,
When proudly we think of their glory
    And the honour their names should receive,
Then we long, with a thrill of elation,
    To blazon their merits afar—
Till we find with intense irritation,
    We are not even told who they are!

So Mr Official 'Eye-Witness',
    When you send those long telegrams through,
We want further proof of your fitness
    For the job they have set you to do.
When the work of brave men who are fighting
    Your special acknowledgement claims,
Just cut out a bit of fine writing,
    And fill up the space with their names!

The Dundee Advertiser, 19 May 1915

Anon

A SOLDIER'S SONG
(From the French)

See these ribbons gaily streaming—
  I'm a soldier now, Lizette!
Yes, of battle I am dreaming
  And the honour I shall get;
With a sabre by my side,
  And a helmet on my brow
And a prancing steed to ride,
  I shall rush upon the foe;
Yes, I flatter me, Lizette,
  'Tis a life that well will suit,
  The gay life of a young recruit.

We shall march away tomorrow,
  At the breaking of the day,
And the trumpets will be sounding,
  And the merry cymbals play;
Yet before I say good-bye
  And a last sad parting take,
As a pledge of your true love,
  Give me kerchief, scarf or glove;
Then cheer up, my Lizette,
  Let not grief your beauty stain—
  Soon you'll see the recruit again.

Shame, Lizette, to thus be weeping
  While there's fame in store for me;
Think, when home I am returning,
  What a joyful day 'twill be!
When to church you're fondly led,
  Like a lady smartly drest,
And a hero you shall wed
  With a medal on his breast;
Oh, there's not a maiden fair,
  But with welcome will salute
  The gay bride of the young recruit.

The Dundee Advertiser, 20 May 1915

Anon

THE GUNNER'S BALLAD

Our happy family consists of three—
The corporal, the bombardier, and me
In various climes it's been our fate to roam,
Till here we find a temporary home.
It isn't furnished in the latest mode,
But then, it's not a permanent abode.

The roof was once, I think, a stable door;
Of straw the carpet that adorns the floor;
The walls are of a quite superior clay,
That sticks to one and won't be lured away.
From off these walls the melting snow is trickling
Adown the corporal's neck—his words are tickling.

We're somewhat limited for space, 'tis true;
If I turn round, so must the other two;
And getting in and out becomes a bore
When one is rather wider than the door;
But still, we're very good at taking cover
When those confounded German souvenirs come over.

'Pass up the pozzy, if it's not all done.'
But hark!—Hi, there, turn out and man your gun!'
There goes the tea, the jam is on the floor;
I'm stuck again—my blessings on this door—
Three thousand yards, corrector 1-4-2,
And 'Fire!'—my German friend, a souvenir for you!

Down falls the night and also falls the rain;
The sentries mount, we seek our home again;
And clinging close the blessèd warmth to keep
Seek sweet oblivion in a dreamless sleep,
Till dawns the day upon the sodden plain
Giving the call to 'Action front!' again.

The People's Journal, 22 May 1915

Anon

THE CALL

Listen once more! The Call
   Beats in the throbbing drum
Bidding not one but all
   Of Britain's manhood come!
Because your comrade went,
   Freely and nothing loth,
Shall all his toil be spent
   To keep you here in sloth?

What use to shut your ears?
   Your country claims her debt,
And in the coming years
   Your heart shall judge you yet!
Think of that future day
   And choose the nobler plan,
That you may truly say
   'At least I played the man!'

The Dundee Advertiser, 2 June 1915

Anon

IN PRAISE OF THE ARMY SERVICE CORPS

He's a hero, Tommy Atkins, and his foes are on the run,
There are tales about his progress, and the victories he
has won;
But when people see the papers and these wondrous tales are
read—
Do they ever think, I wonder, how our soldier lads are fed?

There's another busy soldier, by night as well as day,
On the road to Tipperary he must also find his way,
For when Tommy's in the trenches, amidst the battle's roar,
Who feeds his 'little Mary'? Why, the Army Service Corps.

With the ASC behind them they will never know defeat,
For their hearts are full of courage, and their 'tummies'
full of meat;
So, when the war is over, and the lads come home in glee,
Then, amidst the shouts of welcome, don't forget the ASC.

The People's Journal, 24 July 1915

Anon

A LITTLE FARTHER ON

A little farther on the skies are brighter,
And often scented breezes blow o'er scented fields;
The distant clouds are fleecier and whiter,
And sweeter music o'er the senses steals,
    A little farther on.

A little farther on life is immortal,
Nor pain, nor sorrow ever can molest,
The joys we've missed shall meet us at the portal,
The hands we've loved shall lead us into rest,
    A little farther on.

The People's Journal, 14 August 1915

Anon

PLAY LIFE'S GAME AS MEN

Let's play life's game as men,
　　Let's stand face-front to fate.
Though worsted now and then,
　　Let's not give way to hate.
Let us be brave and bold
　　Whate'er may come our way,
And when the dirge is tolled
　　Above our lifeless clay
Of us let it be said
　　By those who stand and sigh,
A true friend goes ahead,
　　A man is passing by.

Let's play life's game as men,
　　And not as pampered youth;
Knocked down, let's rise again
　　To battle for the truth.
Let's take our share of blows,
　　Though battered, bruised, and faint,
And bear our little woes
　　Sometimes without complaint.
Let us not wail and whine
　　Because our skies are grey,
Heads up, with courage fine,
　　Let's meet what comes our way.

The Dundee Advertiser, 25 August 1915

Anon

FLASH BACK THE SIGNAL

Fall in! Our King and Country are calling
For help for our heroes in dangers appalling,
Let us all—young and old, every woman and man—
Flash back the signal: 'I'll do what I can.'

Remember the children whose fathers have gone!
Remember the mothers that toil all alone!
Remember your duty! each woman! each man!
Remember to do it and to give all you can.

Let us all—young and old: every woman and man—
Flash back the signal: 'I'll do what I can.'

The Dundee Advertiser, 11 September 1915

Anon

STAIN NOT THE SKY

Ye gods of battle, lords of fear,
  Who work your iron will as well
As once ye did with sword and spear,
  With rifle, gun and roaring shell—
Masters of sea and land forbear
The fierce invasion of the inviolate air!

With patient daring man has wrought
  A hundred years for power to fly,
And shall we make his wingèd thought
  A hovering horror in the sky,
Where flocks of human eagles sail
Dropping their bolts of death on hill and dale?

Ah no, the sunset is too pure,
  The dawn too fair, the moon too bright!
For wings of terror to obscure
  Their beauty, and betray the night
That keeps for man above his wars,
The tranquil vision of untroubled stars.

Pass on, pass on, ye lords of fear!
  Your footsteps in the sea are red,
And black on earth your paths appear
  With ruined homes and heaps of dead;
Pass on, and end your transient reign,
And leave the blue of heaven without a stain.

The wrong ye wrought will fall to dust,
  The right ye shielded will abide;
The world at last will learn to trust
  In law to guard, and love to guide;
The peace of God that answers prayer
Will fall like dew from the inviolate air.

The Dundee Advertiser, 28 September 1915

Anon

VICTORY

Only a grave, a coarse hewn grave,
   Only a clumsy mound,
A simple cross to mark the brave
Who in those awful moments gave
Their life, their all, for us to save.
   Sacred this plot of ground.

Only a sigh, a dolorous sigh,
   Only a nation's woe.
A hush'd voice whispers from the sky,
Blest be the souls of them who die
And for the sake of others lie.
   Long may their mem'ry glow.

The Dundee Advertiser, 2 October 1915

15

Anon

THE SOLDIER TO HIS KNAPSACK

You feel he's a friend, tho' he weighs down your back;
You call him a scourge in the day's wear and tear;
You'd leave him behind in the long dusty track—
Yet when there's a halt he provides you a chair.

Beyond on the line where the power of death
Flings wide over all his pestilent seed,
And nerve oozes out with each next-to-last breath,
He serves as a guard to your very life's need.

At times he's your buffet, your larder, your chest,
A furniture suite you can lift in your hand,
Or lay 'neath your head as you curl up to rest
And march in your dreams to a happier land.

'Old fellow, what gruelling days we go through—
What names have I flung at your innocent skin!
I take them all back and swear by the blue
We're pals to the finish through thick and through thin!'

The Dundee Advertiser, 22 November 1915

Anon

THE PIPER OF LOOS

He piped in Scotia's bonny land,
   He piped a sweet Strathspey
He piped in India's coral strand
   A Tullochgorum gay.

He piped a war-charge when at Loos,
   He fell, yet piped he still;
And while this land breeds sturdy thews,
And gallant hearts such strength to use,
And feet that valour's pathway choose,
   His pipes shall Scotland thrill!

The People's Journal, 27 November 1915

Anon

OUR LITTLE DUG-OUT IN THE TRENCHES

We've a cosy little dug-out in the trenches—
　　As cosy as cosy can be;
I'm sorry to say you're too far away,
　　Or we would invite you to tea.

We can't use our fine china tea-cups,
　　Our silver is all packed away
And labelled right on, through to Berlin
　　For long here we don't mean to stay.

But nobody thinks in a dug-out
　　Of knife, fork, or napkin, or plate;
That was no drawback to our party
　　Just here, you'll allow me to state.

The boiled ham we thought was delicious,
　　The butter, oatcakes and the rest,
But the scones baked at home by mother
　　Of all the good things were the best.

We don't walk about in the sunshine,
　　We do all our prowling at night;
We are happy as kings in our dug-out—
　　At any time ready to fight.

So, though you can't come to our party,
　　There's one thing we can do at least—
To say we shall ever be grateful
　　To you for providing the feast.

The Dundee Advertiser, 4 December 1915

Anon

DUNDEE'S OWN

The day you marched away,
   Dundee's Own,
Our hearts were like to break,
   Dundee's Own.
But you smiled away our tears,
And we stifled all our fears,
Changing them to ringing cheers
   For Dundee's Own.

When Neuve Chapelle was o'er,
   Dundee's Own,
We gloried in your deeds,
   Dundee's Own!
For we knew the town's good name
Had been honoured by your fame,
You had bravely played the game
   For Dundee's Own!

But alas our hearts are sad,
   Dundee's Own.
We mourn your sleeping brave,
   Dundee's Own.
Mid the storm of shot and shell
Where the gallant heroes fell
There lie broken hearts as well
   With Dundee's Own.

When victorious you march home,
   Dundee's Own,
To the city proud to call you
   Dundee's Own.
If we're quiet do not wonder.
We are glad, so glad, yet ponder
On the loved ones left out yonder,
   Dundee's Own!

The People's Journal, 11 December 1915

Anon

BATTLE SLEEP

Somewhere, O sun, some corner there must be
   Thou visitest, where down the strand
Quietly, still, the waves go out to sea,
   From the green fringes of a pastoral land.

Deep in the orchard-bloom the roof-trees stand
   The brown sheep graze along the bay,
And through the apple-boughs above the sand
   The bees' hum sounds no fainter than the spray.

There, through uncounted hours declines the day
   To the low arch of twilight's close,
And, just as night about the moon grows grey,
   One sail leans westward to the fading rose.

Giver of dreams, O thou, with scathless wing
   Forever moving through the fiery hail
To flame-seared lids the cooling vision bring,
   And let some soul go seaward with that sail.

The Dundee Advertiser, 14 December 1915

M A

THE SONG OF THE WORKERS

We are working in the shop, we are working in the shed;
We are working, working, working, day and night.
We are turning out the shot, we are turning out the shells
For our brave lads over yonder in the fight;
They are fighting on the land, they are fighting on the sea,
They are fighting, bleeding, dying, that all nations may
            be free;
They are fighting for their country, they are fighting for
            their King,
So we're working, working, working to help our laddies win.

We are working in the factory, we are working in the shop,
We are working, working, working, and we never, never stop,
We are turning out the cloth in bales, and boots in thousands,
            too,
For we're clothing all the khaki lads, and all the boys in blue;
They heard the call of nations and went forth to the fight
To battle for the cause of Truth, of Freedom, Justice, Right.
So we've no room for shirkers, and we've no time for fun,
We want to do our little bit and help to beat the Hun.

We are working in the factory, we are working in the shed,
We are working, working, working that our laddies may be fed.
We're busy tinning jam and meat, and making biscuits too,
For we feed the boys in khaki and the boys in navy blue.
We have no time for shirking, and we have no time for play
For our boys they keep us busy at night as well as day;
So we're working, working, working, for we're men of fun and go.
And mean to do our little bit and help to thrash the foe;

And when we're tired and weary, and ready to give in,
We hear their voices cheery above the battle's din,
They sound across the water in ringing tones so clear,
'Keep sending out the stuff, my boys, we're winning! Do you
            hear?'

'Aye, aye, my lads, we hear it, we'll work till all is done,
With a long pull all together, with steady arms and strong;
We have no room for slackers, and we have no time for play,
Ay, you shall have the stuff, my lads, and you shall win
                                                    the day.'

Oh! Tommy, Jack and Joe, how much to you we owe,
We'll feed you, clothe you, arm you, and help you beat the foe;
And when the conflict's over, the hard-fought battle won,
Our songs of praise to God we'll raise for the victory o'er
                                                    the Hun.

The Dundee Advertiser, 30 May 1915

A C Adie

WATCH AND WARD

See the watch-dogs of the deep,
See them nightly vigils keep!
While the land is locked in sleep,
    There they watch and ward.
All the seasons of the year,
From their watch they never steer,
Save to action with a cheer,
    Sailors clear the board.

Braving winter, braving war,
Angry storms and cannons' roar,
Warding horrors from our shore,
    Yonder German horde!
Thanks to them, who, night and day,
Keep our hell-hound foes at bay,
    They shall have reward.

The Dundee Advertiser, 13 October 1915

D Alexander

MOTHER'S CALL

Where are you going, my boy?
  (Said a mother to her son),
It is surely not to sports,
  When there's brave work to be done.

Your Mother-Country's calling you,
  To help her in her plight;
And surely it's a better game
  To help her in the fight.

My boy, you're not a shirker,
  I'm sure you're good and true;
And that you won't disgrace me,
  When your country calls for you.

The People's Journal, 9 January 1915

Robert T Anderson

THE OLDEST ALLIES IN EUROPE
1295–1915

Here in the low lands of Flanders
When Bourbon or Guise held power,
Came many a lanky Scots lad
From many a northern tower,
With purse that was sore depleted.
But sword that his arm could swing;
O! so came our soldiers of fortune
When Louis Quatorze was king.

And here with the lazy barges
Asleep in the dull canal,
And the tall trim trees a-standing
As Dutch trees ever shall,
The horse-ponds willow-bordered,
And the hop-poles long and spare,
He stayed—but he dreamed of the heather
That scented the Highland air.

He thought of the mountain passes
When the grey mist wrapt them in gloom,
He thought of the shaggy cattle
That stood knee-deep in the broom;
He saw the blue wreath curling
From the cot by the dashing stream,
But he woke to the Flemish farmsteads
And a folk that never dream.

And now we have come to the places
Our Scots lads knew in their day;
The same old windmills are standing,
The same old shrines by the way;
We clatter our horses by causeways,
Old arches resound to the clang,
The half-timid burgher at daylight
But glimpses the troop as we gang.

O! here we are riding in Flanders
Where the diced-band often has been—
The roadways are thronged with soldiers,
And many a one of our kin.
The kilts swing by to the pibroch
Thro' the white dust of the road,
They gang to the trench lighthearted,
As brisk as their fathers strode.

Yet each one thinks of the braeside
His earliest years had kent,
And each has thought for his own lass
And places where oft they went;
And each has a pride in his own heart—
A pride that's no useless thing,
That he stands as stout soldier as any
When Louis Quatorze was king.

When our lads came in the old days
They fought for the pillage and pay;
They rendered their swords to the war-lords—
For men who were richer than they.
But ours that have come into Flanders
Come not for plunder or gain,
But as a bulwark to freedom,
So shall they ever remain.

The Frank as he turns to the battle
And sees the long lines oppose,
Can mind of the Prussian invasion
When his land was trodden by foes,
But his confidence comes with the long lines
Of dusty khaki-clad men,
For the 'Oldest Allies' in Europe
Are now together again.

The Dundee Advertiser, 23 May 1915

A F Arnold

THE HAPPY DEAD

(A Reply to Lance-Corporal Joseph Lee's poem,
'The Green Grass')

They have nobler thoughts, the dead who die
On the red, red fields of France,
Nor mourn, nor turn like a restless child,
    Peaceful they sleep, nor sigh.

We lie at peace in a foreign soil,
In the sweet deep peace of rest from toil,
    Because we nobly died.

We died, though the life we left was sweet,
That wrong might have its payment meet,
    For this we died.

Though the life pulsed strong in our veins of youth,
We laid it down in the cause of truth:
    For this we died.

For wives and bairns 'gainst ruthless power
I strove and fought in that last dread hour.
    For them I died.

I dealt a swifter bayonet thrust,
Lest my sweetheart should suffer brutal lust,
    For her I died.

Our homes from Belgium's fate to save,
Boldly we went to our own red grave,
    And gladly died.

Above our graves the grass grows green,
We lie in deep content serene,
    Because we nobly died.

In the long future of Britain's life, shall our tomb
$$\text{an altar be,}$$
As with those who fought the Persian host, long since
$$\text{at Thermopylae,}$$
For like them we died.

Like them we passed God's keenest test,
Like them we saved from the east, the west:
Like them we died.

We laid down our lives that our friends might live,
The greatest gift that a man can give;
And thus we died.

So we wait in peace till that great Day,
When Christ our Lord, 'Well done,' shall say
To the dead who nobly died.

The Dundee Advertiser, 16 August 1915

Margaret Lee Ashley

THE PLANTING
(Belgium 1915)

Thou patient field where patient dead have lain
Canst feel the soft warm rivers of the rain
    Turn red to green again?

The springy winds call to me: 'Come forth and bring
Thy scanty grain. Once more green blades must spring
    Where death had harvesting.'

Thou lean old steed—too old to feel the knee
Of friend or foe—my child sits lightly, see?
    We two have need of thee.

The plough is broken—patience, little son!
Rest thou thy small, thin legs—too weak to run:
    Dream thou of harvests won.

Yet who shall garner at the summer's close
O little field that grey-clad Sorrow sows?
    God knows—God knows.

The Dundee Advertiser, *21 April 1915*

F B

BRITAIN'S WAR

If we cannot join our brothers
When there beats the martial drum,
And the sounds of strife and conflict
Call on Britain's sons to come;
Yet a duty's laid upon us,
Though the stay-at-homes we are,
For it's shoulder, man, to shoulder
In the time of Britain's war.
We can send our brothers greeting,
From our homes, of love and light,
That our heart's desire and prayers are—
'God be with them in the fight.'
Down with party pride and action
In the hour of Britain's woe,
Each and all to rise and conquer
Those who seek to overthrow
Let them know we still remember
Those who've answered duty's call
In the hour of Britain's danger,
And we mourn for those who fall.
Tell the men who fight the battles,
Who have death and danger braved,
We are with them in the struggle
That the Empire may be saved.
It's not for greed of conquest
That our heroes leave their home;
They've heard a holy summons
In the name of God, to come.
May His righteous anger spare them
Who at first unsheathed the sword;
We would ask forgiveness for them,
And give vengeance to the Lord.
Round the hoary flag of Britain
Black and white together stand,
From the northern snow-clad mountain
Unto India's coral strand.

At the thought our pulses quicken,
Though the stay-at-homes we are,
And we'll stand as one to help them
Who are fighting Britain's war.

The Dundee Advertiser, 5 May 1915

J B B

A MARCHING SONG

Tramp! Tramp! Tramp!
   Through the roar of the city's throng,
The sound you hear is the rhythmic tread
   Of men, as they march along
With lifted head and buoyant heart,
   In the cause of right they go,
Ready to fight, ready to die
   And ready to meet the foe.

Tramp! Tramp! Tramp!
   Go the warriors of the world,
From the Southern Cross and frozen North
   Is Freedom's flag unfurled.
Cries of despair have reach'd them all,
   'Tis a people's shriek of pain,
Woe! woe! to the murdering Hun
   When met on the battle plain!

Tramp! Tramp! Tramp!
   The makers of destiny go,
With hearts aflame for a nation's wrong,
   And rage at a ruthless foe.
Nothing shall stay their arm,
   Nothing shall shake their plan,
Till they tear the 'mark of the beast'
   Away from the face of man.

The Dundee Advertiser, 26 August 1915

James Baker

HERE'S TO THE MEN IN THE TRENCHES

Here's to the men in the trenches,
   The men who have held the line,
And baffled the foe by many a blow,
   Though outnumbered as one to nine.

Here's to the men in the trenches
   The men who, so staunch and true,
Have saved the lives of our children and wives,
   And saved both me and you.

Here's to the men in the trenches,
   Who have saved us from Germany's heel,
And dogged and stern have made the foe learn
   The keenness of British steel.

Here's to the men in the trenches,
   And long may history know them;
In Britain's song as the years roll along,
   God pay them the debt we owe them.

The Dundee Advertiser, 9 March 1915

Armstrong Barry

THE UNBROKEN HOPE

I saw a rainbow rising from the sea
Brief as the soothing summer shower it stayed;
Soon were its colours faded in the air,
But not before this song was left with me:
    On Oceans of the world
    Still sail with flags unfurl'd
    The silent fleets which form
    A brave unbroken arc—
    The rainbow that appears
    To calm a nation's fears.
    Gone is a year of storm
    Yet must they face the dark,
    Threat'ning to overwhelm.
    O trust that at the helm
    Is He who placed the promise in the sky
    Steering to the fair port of victory.

The Dundee Advertiser, 4 August 1915; republished in *Laurel and Myrtle*.

Armstrong Barry

FALLEN
(Poem for those killed at Loos)

A word of Autumn with its with'ring leaves
Which chilling winds drive to a winter grave.
Why should we use it then, regards the brave
Whose loss today a mourning city grieves?
For them no slow decay, nor length'ning eves;
A death like theirs assuredly doth save
From all base colouring, must ever waive
The commonplace, and nought but glory weaves.

A word passing the lips when in the night
Speeds a swift star before consid'ring eyes,
A momentary gleam, forgotten quite
Amid the blazonry that never dies.
Say rather, they have risen and are aye
Fixed stars upon the sky of memory.

The Dundee Advertiser, 6 October 1915; republished in *Laurel and Myrtle*

Armstrong Barry

BROKEN MADONNAS

They are but images of wood or stone,
And yet speak to the soul of tenderness
And love, of little children sweet
That on the Christmas morn did greet
The gentle lady of the shepherd's quest,
But who are now—ah! that God knoweth best.

They tell of broken mothers who are borne
To their own far-off happy Bethlehem
In solemn thought, down mem'ried years,
Who at the Cross, despite their tears,
Sing as true sharers of the piercing sword
A proud Magnificat unto the Lord.

The Dundee Advertiser, 22 December 1915; republished in *Laurel and Myrtle*

D D Beaton

A LILT FOR THE DAY

Hallo! boys, Hallo! Halt! and listen to the cry—
Your King and country need you, and on you rely
To rally round the flag, boys, Scotia's valiant sons,
To fight and to conquer the cowardly brutal Huns.

Chorus

> Then come, let us sing, boys,
> Our grand old refrain—
> We always are ready! Steady, boys, steady!
> We'll fight and we'll conquer again and again.

Our Empire's in danger, our liberty's at stake!
Then forward, boys, defend them! Show the Lion's still
awake
To guard Right and Justice, Honour, Freedom, Fame,
And 'venge such fiendish crimes as stain the Kaiser's name.

Their arrogance, brutality and treachery so base
Have proved the Huns unscrupulous, unworthy as a race!
Their pride must be abased, their ambition deadly hit!
Come boys, help to do it by your sturdy Scottish grit.

We'll win boys, we'll win! Scotsmen never shall be slaves,
For Freedom beams triumphant where'er the tartan waves.
Then don the kilt at once, boys, and shoulder your guns,
And do your bit in smashing the cowardly Huns.

The Dundee Advertiser, 2 December 1915

J R Black

THANKS FOR GIFTS

Your chocolate's eaten long ago;
   Your cigarettes—I've smoked them too;
And here's a line to let you know
   How much I am obliged to you.

For all your wishes, thanks sincere;
   They reached me on a muddy day,
And made me feel that Leslie's near,
   Though Tipperary's far away.

I heard the clatter of the mills,
   The bairns at play on braes and green,
I saw the rounded Lomond hills,
   With peace pervading all the scene.

While in the village where I write,
   Where war has said his cruel say,
There are no ingles blazing bright,
   There are no children left to play.

What once were homes are ruined walls,
   And shells have shattered school and spire;
Amid the stones a lean cat crawls—
   All that's escaped from fend and fire.

May sun ne'er rise upon the day
   When fate shall deal with Leslie so—
That is my wish from far away,
   And here's a line to let you know.

The Dundee Advertiser, 30 January 1915

Sergeant F M Cockburn

KILLIECRANKIE—A NEW VERSION

Whaur cam ye frae, my bonnie lads,
    Whaur cam ye frae sae bankie, O?
O we're the men the Bosches ken,
    The lads o' Killiecrankie, O!

Chorus
And had ye been whaur we hae been,
    Ye wadna craw sae cantie, O!
And had ye seen what we hae seen
    Syn we left Killiecrankie, O!

We've focht in lands across the sea,
    Frae India tae Ashanti, O!
We brocht the Deil and a ' Dundee
    Tae France frae Killiecrankie, O!

The Prussian Guard, we hit them hard
    The Huns they had a clankie, O!
They'll ne'er forget the day they met
    The lads o' Killiecrankie, O!

Then, 'On the ball, Dundee' and all,
    Bring down the Kaiser, swankie, O!
Till we get there, we'll do and dare
    For King and Killiecrankie, O!

The Dundee Advertiser, 13 December 1915

C N Craig

A FEW THOUGHTS IN THE TRENCH

I sat in my dug-out one day,
And I tried to think it out
How I was here, and Fritz was there,
And how it came about.
I thought of home, and folks at home,
And wondered were they well;
But the sand-bag wall beside me
Spoke no word—it could not tell.

I looked beyond the door-outside,
And viewed the grave-plot square;
And asked myself how I was here
And they were—over there?
An' was I lucky, or were they?
'Twas really hard to say;
Yet they'd a chance and paid the price,
And mine was still to pay.

I gazed beyond the graves to where
The trench curved in the night
And thought how many boys of 'Ours'
Would live through the coming night.
An' wondered if the sentry, standing
Periscope in hand,
Could realise how near he was
To the 'immortal band'.

And if he fell would those at home
Grieve sorely for his loss?
Perchance the shot waits next relief,
The coin needs but a toss.
And will he get a grazing wound,
To take him home to care?
Or will his fate deny him thus,
And give him one dead-square?

Oh life is here a slender thing,
So near to death are we;
A hand upraised, a touch prepared,
A touch for you or me.

'Stand to arms! Stand to! Stand to!'
So now it's Fritz and me;
With rifle clean, the bolt well oiled,
My thoughts must cease to be.

The People's Journal, 30 October 1915

C N Craig

'TIS A BEAUTIFUL STREET

'Tis a beautiful street of 'semi-detacheds',
   And the outlook is wide and free
(It may be admitted you exercise care
   If the scene you desire to see).
The villas are cosy, neat and well built,
   And scarcely ever collapse
(Care must be observed when turning about,
   Or you may get interred, perhaps).
The neighbours are cheerful and always agree
   With themselves, but one need not mind that
(There are other annoyances which are much worse
   Amongst folk who exist in a flat).
The rent here is free and the landlord can't give
   One a house any cheaper than this
(But he makes a condition on tenancy terms
   That to 'some' is impossible 'biz').
Firstly and lastly you must be a MAN
   To claim a 'detached' in our street;
And you must dress in khaki and carry a gun—
   Is this an impossible feat?
To 'some' it would seem so, for we have a few
   Vacant villas we'd like occupied,
And from what I remember of Dundee of old,
   There's enough men to keep us supplied.
Then there's Fritz 'cross the way: he'd get a surprise
   If he saw YOU at 'Stand-to' peep o'er;
And don't you consider if YOU fill the gap
   That the war would be shorter some more.

The People's Journal, 27 November 1915

T M Davidson

INVOCATION

God Almighty, make us worthy
Of our Empire yet to be!
May her people serve thee gladly,
Walking humbly in the light,
Hating evil, loving mercy,
Doing justly in Thy sight,
Regarding still a neighbour's needs
More than the shibboleths of creeds.

God Almighty, make us worthy,
Worthy of a lasting peace!
Worthy of our sons and kindred
Who for us their blood have shed.
Worthy of their sacrifices
Worthy of the valiant dead;
O hasten Lord, the time of peace,
When right shall reign and hate shall cease.

God Almighty, make us worthy,
Worthy of thine only Son!
Who for us gave up His glory
That He might to men proclaim
Peace and mercy, love and pity,
Through His birth at Bethlehem;
O hasten, Lord, the time of peace,
When right shall reign and war shall cease.

The Dundee Advertiser, 30 September 1915

Harry M Dean

WAR

A cave man in his dingy cave
 Worked with his knife of bone
Until he drew an arrow true,
 Tipping the shaft with stone.
His woman stood close by his side
 To loop the long bow string;
For dawn's dim light would bring the fight,
 Bring war, the deadly thing.

A star, swung high above the plain,
Shed pale light on the heaped-up slain.

A knight all clad in shining mail
 Rode forth to join his band;
His sword was new, but deadly true,
 When wielded by his hand.
His lady-love was there to see
 Her lover ride away;
And then to yearn for his return
 With honours from the fray.

Sunrise staining the east with gold,
And upturned faces grey and cold.

Long lines of men with guns steel-tipped
 Marched on and ever on,
From morning light until the night—
 From night till blood-red dawn.
Behind, the women prayed and wept
 For Him to heed their cries;
But naught could stay them on their way—
 Poor human sacrifice.

Long low hills and the slanting sun,
And fields all red when the fight is done.

The Dundee Advertiser, 7 March 1915

Draycott M Dell

REQUIEM

A shot—a boom of guns afar—
The angry utterances of war,
The sunrays through the pines come creeping
Like tiny children—timorous—peeping
At our poor slain who, sleeping, lie
Clad in their cloaks—and Majesty.

A bugle note, a distant drum,
Faint 'En Avants' that bid us come;
We lay our relics by the dead,
No word is said, no tear is shed,
A flower or so, and nothing more,
Save just the last salute of war.

The Dundee Advertiser, 27 May 1915

Draycott M Dell

THE BLINDED SOLDIER

Oh! poor, blinded and maimed in the midst of God's wonderful
world,
Filled with the scent of flowers, gay with its flags unfurled,
Wanting a hand to aid, seeking a way to live.
Hark! the blind soldier is calling. What are you going to give?

Will you give a ring or a necklace, a cheque or a falling tear?
Will you give a hand to help one who is waiting here?
Will you lend him the eyes to see with, assist to make him
whole?
A blinded brother—a soldier, soul of your inmost soul.

Cheers will not keep him going; tears he cannot see.
Proud, he would never ask ought of your charity.
Come, from the deep of your pocket, come, from the love in your
heart—
He gave his eyes for England—what is to be your part?

The Dundee Advertiser, 5 November 1915

J B Dollard

THE BATTLE LINE

Athwart that land of blossoming vine
Stretches the awful battle-line;
A lark hangs singing in the sky,
With sullen shrapnel bursting nigh
Along the poplar-bordered road
The peasant trudges with his load,
While horsemen and artillery
Rush to red fields that are to be!
The plains for tillage furrowed well
Are now replowed with shot and shell!
The ditches, swollen by the rain,
Show bloated faces of the slain.
The hedge-rows sweet with leaf and flower
Now mark the cannon's murderous power!
Small birds by household cares opprest
Beg truce and time to build their nest.
The sun sinks down—oh, blest release!
And the spent world cries out for peace.
In vain! In vain! Tho' mild stars shine
War wakes the thundering battle-line.

The Dundee Advertiser, 1 July 1915

Bandmaster Etherington 2/5th RSF

TO BUGLER GOLDEN, BROUGHTY FERRY

Have you been at Broughty Ferry,
   That spot so bright and fair?
Have you rambled on the sea beach
   And felt the briny air?
As the summer sun was sinking
   Beyond the far green west?
That's the home of Bugler Golden,
   The spot he loves the best.

For some would, and some could,
   And some wish they had won it;
But Bugler o' the Twenty-First,
   God bless his heart—he's done it!

Far away in Gallipoli,
   'Midst the screaming of the shell,
Where the Twenty-First are playing
   The game they know so well,
The gallant Bugler Laddie
   Joins in the deadly strife
And saves a wounded comrade
   At the risk of his own life.

For some would, and some could,
   And some wish they had done it;
But the soldier son of a soldier dad,
   He has played the game and won it!

Ah, God, who rules the nations,
   And the children to me born,
Grant mine may be like Golden—
   I would not grudge to mourn
A fallen son; 'twere better
   In Honour's cause to fall,
Than live a craven coward,
   Who dare not hear the call.

For some would, and some could,
   And some wish they had won it;
But the Bugler of the Fusiliers,
   God bless him—for he's done it!

The People's Journal, 28 August 1915

K M F

SHALL SORROW REIGN

Shall sorrow hold the pride of place
   Within our hearts when heroes fall?
And joy, affrighted, hide her face,
   The while we drink unmingled gall.

Though joy takes wing, shall not our pride
   In dauntless deeds yet soothe the pain?
To know they've ventured death's dark tide
   Have given their lives—and not in vain.

And that today as heretofore,
   The foe their prowess does regret—
The valour of their sires of yore,
   That Britain's sons shall ne'er forget.

Let sorrow yield her sullen sway,
   Sweet resignation! lend thy balm;
Thy reign shall be but for a day,
   Oh, grief! give way to holy calm.

The People's Journal, 23 January 1915

G

THE MOTHER

When the weary day is ended,
And the darkness comes again,
In the dead of night I shall meet him,
And my heart will cease its pain.

For he comes—each night he comes to me,
And I wait for the singing grate,
For his footsteps on the staircase—
In the dead of night I wait.

And when on the lonely silence
The bounding footsteps break,
I know not if I'm sleeping,
And I know not if I wake.

For sudden his arms are round me,
And his eyes smile into mine,
And my heart nigh stops with gladness
As my arms about him twine.

Oh, God! with cruel dawning
Comes a vision that sears my brain,
And my heart knows the bitter anguish
Of its reawakened pain.

But the long day has its ending,
And the darkness comes at last—
In the dead of night I shall meet him,
And my arms will hold him fast.

The Dundee Advertiser, 22 May 1915

N H

TO JOSEPH LEE
DUNDEE'S BATTLE BARD

When 'wonder-bird' forsook its nest
  To cheer the warrior's vigil long,
You surely caged it in your breast
  To sing your ballads sweet and strong.

Each theme a tributary makes
  To swell a flow of music sweet;
Each scene a subtler beauty takes,
  A rhythm, from its warm heart-beat.

'Mid scenes of pain and strife you sing
  The sad refrain, the playful air,
With throb and thrill of life they ring
  Yet with no discord of despair.

There where a fallen hero lies,
  A victim of unholy strife,
You gazed on him through spirit eyes,
  That see the inwardness of life.

And sighed, because you had no tears—
  Eyes may be dry through grief's excess—
Now crystallised your grief appears
  In tear-word gems of tenderness.

When 'Mac' prepared his Palace grand—
  As seen through magic of your pen—
No royal house was ever planned
  That sheltered nobler, kinglier men.

They stand, a living wall, between
  Their country and a treacherous foe;
They fight for honour, King and Queen,
  Till their last drop of blood shall flow;

For King and Queen, who nobly stand
　　For Manhood and for Womanhood,
In this their well-belovèd land,
　　Upholders of the true and good.

Brave heart, among the brave and true,
　　Through dark days singing valiantly,
God grant your comrades and to you,
　　Courage and faith and victory.

All through this warfare's tortuous way,
　　May 'wonder-bird' within your breast,
Sing you an angel's melody,
　　Of home and Heaven, of peace and rest.

The Dundee Advertiser, 2 August 1915

Alanson Hartpence

DEFIANCE

Let life its legioned army throw
  Against my pennoned castle walls,
With curse and gibe and bitter groan
  Its band of lowly seneschals.

But when the dust of conflict blows
  And sounds the bugle o'er the lea,
They shall not find me fallen dead:
  They shall not kill the love in me!

Though stained with blood of bleeding heart,
  Up in the ramparts' evening breeze,
My banner floats the same as yore
  Above the brooding cypress trees.

The sun has set; the shadows fade;
  The night comes silent from the sea;
They shall not find me fallen dead;
  They shall not kill the love in me.

The Dundee Advertiser, 14 January 1915

Highland Laddie

FOR THOSE THAT ARE LEFT BEHIND

Come, rally round the banner, boys,
    The red, white, and blue,
Let us show this selfish world
    That our loyal hearts are true.
We do not fight for fortune,
    But for peace and right combined;
'Tis a record of our honour
    That our heroes leave behind.

While we pray the God of Battles
    To give us the victor's song,
And so haste the end of conflict,
    And the day of peace prolong,
We pray that He may help us
    To be bountiful and kind
To the homeless and the helpless
    That our heroes leave behind.

A mite will be accepted boys,
    For a million mites are wealth
To the homeless and the weary
    Who maintained the Empire's strength.
And those who go to battle boys,
    May go with peaceful mind,
For they know we'll guard the welfare
    Of dear ones left behind.

It takes courage for a mother
    To send forth her only son;
And to face the months of waiting
    For the dreaded news to come.
For the sisters and the sweetheart,
    For the wife with babes to mind;
Oh, they're brave and patriotic
    Whom our heroes leave behind.

Let's all be patriotic, boys,
　　And bear the brunt together;
Let's guard the Empire's honour, boys,
　　By helping one another.
While we sing the soldier's glory
　　Let us ever bear in mind
War brings sorrow to the loved ones
　　Whom our heroes leave behind.

The People's Journal, 2 January 1915

D Horne

ONLY A GRAVE IN FLANDERS

Just a grave in blood-stained Flanders,
Heaped up roughly, clods and stones;
A rude cross; yes! just a lance shaft
Set up there to mark the bones
Of him who died for you and me,
And for sacred Liberty!

O' 'tis more! a glorious Dayspring's
Breaking yonder; soon its beams
Shall gleam o'er a risen Belgium,
Shall begild red-ruined Rheims
In Freedom's splendour; and the sea
Will sing of boundless liberty!

Countless, freeborn, mighty legions,
Gather there in sunny France;
Staunch of heart and firm of purpose;
With one thought—to break the trance
Of Death, which holds sweet Liberty
In chains of cruel infamy!

O, ye mighty unsung heroes!
Ye who loved us all so well
That ye lay in blood-stained trenches
And did storm the gates of hell:
Bright shall be your memory
In the days of Liberty!

Shame on us if we forget you!
Ye who lie in nameless graves;
Shame on us if all our Freemen
Be enthralled, and cruel waves
Engulf once more sweet Liberty,
Or blot out your memory.

The Dundee Advertiser, 13 April 1915

Reginald Horsley

A SOLDIER'S PRAYER

Let me not die till one brave deed is set
   Against my name on the eternal page.
Let me not die till this is done, and yet
   Let me not live a losing war to wage.

Let me not live to strive and never win.
   Let me not live in craven fear to run.
Let me not die within the trench of sin.
   Let me not live, my work ignobly done.

Let me not die till Might is slain by Right.
   Let me not live to throw my armour down.
How could I live and living, lose this fight?
   How can I die and, dying, lose my crown?

Yet give me leave to live, if I may be
   Bound in life's bundle with my Lord to lie:
But if to live means dying far from Thee,
   Then save my soul, O God, and let me die.

The Dundee Advertiser, 11 October 1915

Arthur Hougham

HOPE

Though I told my heart to break
  When they said that for his King
    He had died;
Though all night I lay awake
  And I kissed and hid his ring;
    Though I cried.

Like an ivory rose apart,
  Under a gleam of slender moon,
    Scented sweet,
Hope is listening in my heart
  To a nightingale's glad tune:
    We shall meet.

The Dundee Advertiser, 2 November 1915

Walter C Howden

'ONE SHALL BE TAKEN'

O brother mine, O comrade dead,
  O sunny-hearted son,
What wreath to crown your comely head
  When valour claims her own?
Brother o' mine, 'twas ever yours
  To win the favoured goal;
You had the courage that endures,
  The great all-conquering soul.

'Twas yours to join the great crusade,
  'Twas mine to creep along;
And while you flashed a radiant blade,
  I spun an empty song.
'Twas yours to take the high lone road,
  As mine to take the low;
And the proud charger you bestrode
  Went where the god-led go.

I envy you, O brother o' mine,
  Your great glad hour of strife—
Your glorious end! Ah, how supine
  Seems my inglorious life!
Your gallant charge—your dauntless lead—
  Your supreme sacrifice—
These be a heritage, indeed,
  Of deathless memories!

O brother mine, O comrade dead,
  O loyal-hearted son,
What wreath more meet for your dear head
  Than the proud love you've won?
And for your requiem, ours to sing,
  And that triumphantly—
For you, O Death, where is thy sting?
  Grave, where thy victory?

The Dundee Advertiser, 4 October 1915

Frank H Hunby

TO THE LADS

O sons of Scotland! valiant, true,
   Who nobly serve at duty's call,
A nation's heart goes out to you,
   A people's prayers ascend for all.

O Mothers' sons with hearts so brave,
   Alert and keen to play a part,
And take your place on field or wave—
   For you with pride beats Empire's heart.

To you engaged in struggle dire,
   So long drawn out in trenches drear;
Lit up by warfare's raging fire,
   While ghastly death is ever near!

To you on gory battlefields,
   'Mid cannon's roar and bursting shell;
Where death his sharp-set sickle wields
   And plenteous harvest reaps too well!

To you who serve with watchful fleet,
   On treach'rous seas your vigil keep,
All eager there the foe to meet,
   And then to action swiftly leap!

Into your hands doth Britain yield
   Her rightful cause, her Empire's fate;
And countless hearts for you a shield
   By yearning pray'r would fain create.

To you who at the base await
   The word to move on battle line:
Or serve right well at Empire's gate
   If duty's call doth there assign.

To you at home who guard our shore,
  Or now in camp, on training ground,
With keenest zest for war prepare,
  And soon efficient will be found.

To one and all! so valiant, true,
  Who nobly serve at duty's call—
A nation's heart goes out to you,
  A people's prayers ascend for all.

The Dundee Advertiser, 13 January 1915

J W Jack

THE ROSES OF WAR
(After the French of Jacques Normand)

O'er Europe's wide fields dark Terror is spread.
'Tis the gallop of Death in a sky bloody-red,
'Tis the howling of Fury, the foaming of Hate,
And the lives of the Free are being crushed 'neath the
    weight.

On earth and in air, from the West to the East,
The foeman hath sunk to the depth of the beast,
Till stricken with loathing, with shame and disgrace,
Humanity writhes o'er the wrongs of her race.

But amid earth's alarms and the fear that o'erspreads,
See! Courage and Charity lift up their heads.
Bedewed by earth's tears, like rain from on high,
These roses of war raise their blooms to the sky.

The Dundee Advertiser, 29 November 1915

William Johnston

TO JOSEPH LEE

Dear Joseph Lee, I'm glad tae see—
    Tho' times are no' sae rosy—
That ye hae still the he'rt an will
    Tae send us screeds o' poesy;
I'm blest if I—an' mair forbye—
    Can understand hoo ye
Can coort th' muse whaur Hell's let loose,
    An hunders daily dee.

Some sheltered nook beside a brook,
    Or 'neath a shady tree,
Is whaur I gang, when days are lang,
    Tae let my fancy flee;
While near at hand a feathered band
    Strikes up a melody,
Tae help my rhyme, an' a' the time
    Tae fill my he'rt wi' glee.

Sae, Joe, if I were sent oot bye
    To whaur you chance tae be,
I'm safe tae guess the printin' press
    Wad get nae poems frae me;
Th' first big shell that near me fell
    Wad scatter far an free,
If no' my brains, what there remains
    O' rhymin' art in me.

I picture you, lad, tryin' tae woo
    The muse in your dug-oot,
Amid the hail o' shot an' shell,
    That maun be fleein' aboot;
Somehoo I think you'll hae tae juik
    Whene'er you hear a-comin'
A German shell, tae break the spell,
    An' set your lugs abummin'.

My wish is this—that they'll aye miss
   The poet frae auld Dundee,
That you'll come hame no' even lame,
   But wearin' a VC.
My blessin' true I send tae you,
   An' houp that day tae see,
When I will tak' a hearty shak'
   An' somethin' else wi' thee.

The Dundee Advertiser, 13 July 1915

Josephine

THE WOMAN'S PRAYER

Only a tender blossom,
    Wafted down from above,
Crumpled baby fingers,
    God's crown of human love.

Only a brave young hero,
    Longing to do his share,
Yearning, heart-wrung parents,
    And maiden, passing fair.

Only a grave in Flanders,
    Nameless, perhaps—who knows?
Stricken hearts in England,
    The mem'ry of life's rose.

Only a tender blossom,
    Wafted down from above,
'God in Heav'n have mercy,
    Have mercy on our love!'

The Dundee Advertiser, 12 October 1915

Joseph Leckie

THE CUPAR MINISTER'S WAR HYMN

Alleluia! Alleluia! Alleluia!

In battle hour we cry to Thee,
O Father of Eternity,
The Lord and Refuge of the free,
    God Almighty!

The warring standards rise and fall,
The nations hear the thunder-call;
But Thou art silent over all,
    God Almighty!

Beneath Thy pure and awful eyes,
Thou only just and only wise,
We tread the way of sacrifice,
    God Almighty!

Oh, in Thy tender mercy save
From crafty foe and cruel wave,
The young, the hopeful, and the brave
    God Almighty!

Be Thou the light of those who weep
For soldiers dead, that lonely sleep
In stranger land beyond the deep
    God Almighty!

We would be strong to face the fight,
As those who battle for the right,
Yet humble in Thy holy sight,
    God Almighty!

Oh, cleanse us in our secret ways
From all the things of our dispraise,
The rust of unheroic days,
    God Almighty!

Till ends the strife, till sleeps the sword,
When peace and righteousness accord,
Be Thou our strength, Eternal Lord,
    God Almighty!

The Dundee Advertiser, 7 February 1915

Joseph Lee

SOLDIER, SOLDIER

Wastrel, wastrel, standing in the street,
Billy-cock upon your head; boots that show your feet.

Rookie, rookie, not too broad of chest,
But game to do your bloomin' bit with the bloomin' best.

Rookie, rookie, growling at the grub;
Loth to wash behind the ears when you take your tub.

Rookie, rookie, licking into shape—
Thirty-six inch round the buff showing by the tape.

Rookie, rookie, boots and buttons clean;
Mustachios waxing stronger; military mien.

Rookie, rookie, drilling in the square,
Britain's ancient glory in your martial air.

Rookie, rookie, swagger-stick to twirl;
Waving hands to serving-maids; walking out the girl.

Soldier, soldier, ordered to the front,
Marching forward eager-eyed, keen to bear the brunt.

Soldier, soldier, bidding her good-bye—
'When I come back I'll marry you, so, darling, don't
                                                you cry!'

Soldier, soldier, sailing in the ships,
Cigarettes and curious oaths betwixt your boyish lips.

Soldier, soldier, standing in the trench;
Wading through the mud and mire, stifling in the stench.

Soldier, soldier, 'mid the din and dirt,
More than monastic tortures moving in your shirt.

Soldier, soldier, facing shot and shell;
Jesting as you gaze within the open Gate of Hell.

Soldier, soldier, charging on the foe,
With your comrade's dying cry to urge you as you go.

Soldier, soldier, stilly lying dead,
With a dum-dum bullet through your dunderhead.

Soldier, soldier, with a smile of grace,
Breaking through the grime and grit on your blood-swept
                                                    face.

Soldier, soldier, sound will be your sleep,
You will never waken, though you hear her weep.

Soldier, soldier—
        How I love you!

The People's Journal, 17 July 1915; republished in *Ballads of Battle*

Joseph Lee

THE GREEN GRASS

The dead spake together last night,
   And one to the other said:
   'Why are we dead?'

They turned them face to face about
   In the place where they were laid:
   'Why are we dead?'

'This is the sweet, sweet month o' May,
   And the grass is green o'erhead—
   Why are we dead?

'The grass grows green on the long, long tracks
   That I shall never tread—
   Why are we dead?

'The lamp shines like the glow-worm spark,
   From the bield where I was bred—
   Why am I dead?'

The other spake: 'I've wife and weans,
   Yet I lie in this waesome bed—
   Why am I dead?'

'O, I hae a wife and weans at hame,
   And they clamour loud for bread—
   Why am I dead?

Quoth the first: 'I have a sweet, sweetheart,
   And this night we should hae wed—
   Why am I dead?

'And I can see another man
   Will mate her in my stead,
   Now I am dead.'

They turned them back to back about
    In the grave where they were laid—
    'Why are we dead?'

'I mind o' a field, a foughten field,
    Where the bluid ran ruth and red
    Now I am dead.'

'I mind o' a field, a stricken field,
    And a waeful wound that bled—
    Now I am dead.'

They turned them on their backs again,
    As when their souls had sped,
    And nothing further said.

The dead spake together last night,
    And each to the other said,
    'Why are we dead?'

The Dundee Advertiser, 6 August 1915; republished in *Ballads of Battle*

Joseph Lee

THE BULLET

Every bullet has its billet;
  Many bullets more than one:
God! perhaps I killed a mother
  When I killed a mother's son.

The Dundee Advertiser, 24 September 1915; republished in *Ballads of Battle*

Joseph Lee

THE BROKEN HEART

I found a silver sixpence,
A sixpence, a sixpence,
I found a silver sixpence,
   And I brake it in twa;
I gied it till a sodger,
A sodger, a sodger,
I gied it till a sodger,
   Before he gaed awa'.

I have a heart that's broken,
That's broken, that's broken;
I bear a heart that's broken,
   That's broken in twa—
For I gied it till a sodger
A sodger, a sodger,
I gied it till a sodger,
   Before he gaed awa'!

The Dundee Advertiser, 5 October 1915; republished in *Ballads of Battle*

Joseph Lee

MARCHING

Marching, marching,
  On the old-time track;
     Soldier song upon my lip,
     Haversack upon my hip,
  Pack upon my back;
     Linton on my left hand,
On my right side Jack—
Marching, marching,
     Steel swung at my thigh,
Marching, marching,
     Who so gay as I?

                           (Left, left!)

Marching, marching,
  On the same old track;
     Sorrow gnawing at my heart,
     Mem'ry piercing like a dart,
  Care perched on my back;
     Linton on my left hand—
But, alas! poor Jack!
Marching, marching,
     Quietly does he lie,
Marching, marching,
     Who so sad as I?

                     (Left, left—*LEFT!*)

The Dundee Advertiser, 14 October 1915; republished in *Ballads of Battle*

Joseph Lee

LA CROIX ROUGE

Two thousand years since Christ was crucified;
    Since thorn and nail did torment that frail flesh:
        Again I see
        Him hangèd on a tree,
    And crucified afresh!

Once more that darkness over all the land;
    The graves—*the graves are full*—they give not up their dead:
        The bitter cup
        Is lifted up,
    The crown pierces His head.

The scourging rod, the mocking reed are His,
    The veritable Son of Man and God;
        Through feet and hands
        The iron stands,
    The Cross is red with blood.

Barabbas is released unto the World;
    The thieves—*The thieves are unrepentant both*—
        With swords and staves
        A crowd of knaves
    Come forth with jest and oath.

Again the brutal soldiery cast lots;
    The earth is rent with wrath, and rack, and rue,
        Comes like a sigh
        That lonely cry:
    'They know not what they do!'

Thou Kaiser, who hast crucified thy Christ;
    Judas, Pilatus, Peter—three in one!
        Who shall it be
        Shall say to thee:
    Servant, thy work well done?

For thirty pieces Judas sold his Lord,
   And Peter but denied his Master thrice;
      And Pilate stands
      With washen hands—
   Princeling, what was thy price?

Better, O Caesar—Caiphas, High Priest,
   With all thy servile Scribes and Pharisees—
      Thou'dst ne'er been born
      Than put to scorn
   One of the least of these!

Proud Kaiser, who has drowned the world in tears,
   And deluged all the earth with reddest rain—
      Christ's brow is torn
      With crown of thorn—
   Thine bears the brand of Cain!

O King in name, who might have been in deed,
   Who chose the darkness rather than the light:
      I see thee go
      Forth from thy foe
   And it is night!

The Dundee Advertiser, 24 December 1915; republished in *Ballads of Battle*

G MacG

TO LANCE-CORPORAL JOSEPH LEE
(1/4th Battalion, Black Watch)

For lang months bye, at intervals
The magic of your madrigals
   Has thrilled us through;
And aye we ask for more and more
Frae Joseph Lee's poetic store—
   Is't aye brim fu'?

Or does it sometimes fa' fell low:
The fickle Muse, does she say No
   Tae your request?
Puir lass, nae doot she's aften tired;
Frae sichts and soonds o' big guns fired
   She'll need a rest.

Be mindfu' o' her, Joseph Lee,
Brave sojer frae auld Dundee—
   An' for yersel',
God gaird ye whaur ere ye stand
On duty in that troubled land
   O' shot an' shell.

The Dundee Advertiser, 7 September 1915

Murdoch Maclean

NO MORE

The cloud-wrack o'er the sullen sea is flying
    And the mist hoar,
The night winds in their ocean caves are sighing
    For evermore,
And the thousand voices of the deep are crying
    By the lone shore,
But Angus never turns him home again to Morven.

The browsing flocks upon the hillside roaming
    Have sought the crest,
The lowing kine have left the field as gloaming
    Fades in the west,
And down the vale the wind-tossed bee is homing
    To its long rest,
Yet Angus never turns him home again to Morven.

For out beneath the war-clouds redden'd awning
    Where Fate is nigh,
Where hearts are steel'd, and eager steeds are fawning
    And brave men die,
He softly sleeps, nor wakes to see the dawning
    In the grey sky,
And ocean voices wail his coronach in Morven.

The Dundee Advertiser, 16 July 1915

Alexander M'Leish

A PRAYER

Thou who art greater far than wind or wave,
A suppliant People calls upon Thy name;
Oh! keep us clean from infamy and shame—
E'en though our path is shadowed by the grave!
Lord of all Peoples! Thine each victory won,
Thou, who a very King, yet came to save,
And laid Thy life on Calvary's silent Hill.
Oh! grant us of that love Ye freely gave
And keep us humble and obedient still—
That we may serve Thee as our sires have done;
Then, though the Tempest shake life's ebbing sands
And War's dread blast sweep onward far and free,
Thou wilt uplift us with Thy sinless hands:
We would go forward, loving, serving Thee.

The Dundee Advertiser, 21 January 1915

Alexander M'Leish

LA BASSEE: AN INCIDENT

Rent and shattered by their cannon,
   Scorched by every burning breath,
There we paused one blinded moment
   In the very vale of Death!
Then as moved by one great impulse
   That we could not understand,
Through that hail of leaden horror
   Burst our dauntless Highland band.

Fiercer sang the shot about us,
   Sounding many a hero's knell,
And the winter snow was reddened
   With the cannon's belching hell.
Then a comrade in the forefront
   Rang the slogan call we knew—
'Scotland! Scotland!' How we loved it,
   And it thrilled us through and through!

Every German saw and wonder'd,
   As we grimly struggled on,
For they knew not what had thrilled us
   In the fearful battle zone
'Twas the thunder'd name of 'Scotland!'
   Dear wherever Scotsmen roam,
And it swept us on to glory,
   Like a message sent from home.

The Dundee Advertiser, 10 February 1915

Alexander M'Leish

THE OLD ROAD

(The old road of honour and glory, which we again tread
for our country's sake)

The old road, the old road,
    That winds we know not where—
O, who will take the old road
    With courage strong to dare?
Though sorrow's on the old road,
    Before the day is done,
Far out upon the old road
    There's glory to be won!

The old road, the old road,
    That rings the summer through;
There's something on the old road
    That love enshrines for you!
O bonnie is the old road
    Comes winding down the glen—
There's music on the old road
    And tramp of armèd men.

The old road, the long road,
    We've loved it many a day;
Out there upon the old road
    We've kept our foes at bay.
Along the dreary old road
    The gage of battle's thrown;
God guide us on the old road
    And keep it for our own.

Your country is the old road,
    Where men shall play their part—
The old road, the dear road,
    That winds through every heart,
Our fathers trod the old road,
    'Twas bought with blood and pain;
God with us, on the old road,
    We'll pay the price again.

The Dundee Advertiser, 11 June 1915

J. M'Lellan

A CHEERY BIT LETTER FRAE HAME

Oh, a cheery bit letter frae hame,
Jist a welcome bit screed frae a frien',
Mak's life worth livin', dull moments a heaven,
And lessens the distance between
The darling old homeland and here,
The spot that to us is so dear;
Oh, my heart fills wi' glee when I'm faur ower the sea,
At the thocht o' a letter frae hame.

Jist a cheery bit letter frae hame
Helps Tommy to conquer the foe;
A cheery bit letter is gey often better
Than a' the great doctors I know.
Remember your Tommy or Jack,
May never be spared to come back,
So remember the boys, share their sorrows and joys
In a cheery bit letter frae hame.

It's a cheery bit letter frae hame
That mak's us forget and forgive;
It pierces the bubbles o' family troubles,
An' mak's us in harmony live;
It brings back to memory dear
The scenes o' oor youth and guid cheer.
Oh, it's certainly nice to get hamely advice
In a cheery bit letter frae hame.

The Dundee Advertiser, 18 October 1915

James McNally

SWORD AND PEN

Ancient among the feuds, never before
Did his fell strife so menace as today—
This duel to the death with mind at bay
And might in perfect fettle, fierce of roar,
Roused by low passion and the lust of gore,
The ruthless Sword, forcing the awesome fray,
Seems destined to the hilt to have its way—
Seems verging on the role of conqueror.
Courage! Above the crimson river's flow,
Above the ravaged homes and ruined land,
Justice and love outlive Hate's wildest gust;
The Pen supreme shall yet subdue the foe—
Shall doom, by man's consent and God's command,
The reeking sabre to eternal rust!

The Dundee Advertiser, 3 November 1915

D M

EUROPE'S CARD PLAYERS

Nap (European)
I'll go one, says Belgium,
I'll go two, says France;
I'll go three, says Russia
If I ever get the chance;
I'll go four, says Germany,
And wipe them off the map,
But they all dropped dead when John Bull said
I'm d—— if I don't go nap.

Euchre (European)
Belgium led off Aces,
France replied with Kings,
Russia played the left Bower
To see what cards it brings;
Germany played the right Bower,
And said I am no mocker,
But they all fell flop when down on top
Old John Bull played the Jocker.

The Dundee Advertiser, 31 January 1915

85

W D M

OOR GALLANT FOURTH

Lads o' valour, lads o' grit,
Lads whas' frames are strongly knit,
Lads wha strike hard whom they hit,
      Are in the Fourth.

The 'Great Push' found them tae the fore,
Like their sires in days of yore.
'Marmalade!' Eh, what a roar!
      Cam' frae the Fourth.

They cared not for the rifles' spit,
They were oot tae dae their bit,
They've proved that they are lads o' grit,
      Oor gallant Fourth.

'On the ba', Dundee', they cried
They as steel in fire were tried,
Nobly lived and nobly died,
      Lads o' the Fourth.

When o' worldly cares I'm free,
And I've crossed the 'sullen sea',
Weel tae the fore I ken I'll see
      Lads o' the Fourth.

The People's Journal, 16 October 1915

Mater Militis

MOTHER TO MOTHERS: AN APPEAL

You say you love your son too well
   To bid him go to fight—
To face the German shot and shell
   Where Wrong is throttling Right?

Think you those mothers who have sent
   Their sons to face the foe,
Felt not their souls with anguish rent
   E'en while they bade them 'Go!'

O Blind to Duty's finger-post,
   And Deaf to Duty's call,
Let fear bestir you, lest the host
   Barbarian on us fall.

Here in our peaceful sheltered Land,
   Shattering homes and—worse!—
Too late, ah, then, to make a stand;
   Huns heed nor prayer nor curse!

'Be British!' Heed your Country's call,
   Act not the Alien's part!
God keep your Boy, whate'er befall;
   And His Peace keep your heart!

The Dundee Advertiser, 4 September 1915

Edna Mead

AT WINTER'S END

I flung my eastern casement open wide
To meet the March moon climbing close outside,
Cross-barred by dark-drawn spires of lofty pines,
Its flood of silver struggling through the screen
Of their impenetrable evergreen.
Deeply I drank a draught of cold fresh air
While in my soul rebellion rose that Spring
Should come to strip the heart of Winter bare.
I held my hands out to the gleaming night,
Bidding it, 'Stay, forever! ne'er take flight
Into lethargic lilac-scented dawns;
I bear no love for April nor for May
I have no wish to watch their stars nor share
That warmth of a moist midnight earth they bring;
I want no meadows with pale primrose pied;
I cling fast to the folded fields that hide
Below their frosts and unforgotten face.
Spring? Ah, it may be well for those who hear
The light lark song of Love's young burgeoning!
But my love lies asleep in calm repose,
Untroubled underneath the brooding snows
Of an old, outgrown year.
A strange peace wraps me, while no bird-note strays
To stir my grief-numbed soul to anguished life.
Winter is kind and strong and sane and true,
His brave skies clearly blue,
Uplift my thought, encourage my intent.
His winds have found me fearless; I can meet
Gladly his glittering host of visioned days,
His jewelled nights, with deep white moons ablaze;
Happy, I haste to trudge some storm-swept mile
Where the crisp, crunching tune of crystal flakes
Makes music 'neath my onward spurring feet,
So I forget my dead—a little while.

*   *   *

But—and my hands fall heavy, gripping tight
Against the window-ledge!—how shall I fight
The tide o'erwhelming, of my deep despair?
When all the earth lies open: when the flowers
Send forth fresh shoots—the days new hours—
And Love, for others, breathes and lives again,
While to my farthest call no echo wakes,
My dreams are spent in vain,
And my heart breaks!

The Dundee Advertiser, 13 April 1915

Ruth Comfort Mitchell

BILLY, THE SOLDIER BOY

He marched away with a blithe young score of him
  With the first volunteers,
Clear-eyed and clean and sound to the core of him,
  Blushing under the cheers.
They were fine new flags that swung a-flying there,
Oh, the pretty girls he glimpsed a-crying there,
  Pelting him with pinks and with roses—
    Billy, the Soldier Boy.

Not very clear in the kind young heart of him
  What the fuss was about,
But the flowers and the flags seemed part of him—
  The music drowned his doubt.
It's a fine, brave sight they were a-coming there
To the gay, bold tune they kept a-drumming there,
  While the boasting fifes shrilled jauntily—
    Billy, the Soldier Boy!

Soon he is one with the blinding smoke of it—
  Volley and curse and groan;
Then he has done with the knightly joke of it—
  It's rending flesh and bone.
There are pain-crazed animals a-shrieking there
And a warm blood stench that is a-reeking there;
  He fights like a rat in a corner—
    Billy, the Soldier Boy!

There he lies now, like a ghoulish score of him,
  Left on the field for dead.
The ground all round is smeared with the gore of him—
  Even the leaves are red.
The Thing that was Billy lies a-dying there,
Writhing and a-twisting and a-crying there,
  A sickening sun grins down on him—
    Billy, the Soldier Boy!

Still not quite clear in the poor wrung heart of him
    What the fuss was about;
See where he lies—or a ghastly part of him—
    While life is oozing out:
There are loathsome things he sees a-crawling there,
There are hoarse-voiced crows he hears a-calling there,
    Eager for the foul feast spread for them—
        Billy, the Soldier Boy!

How much longer, O Lord! shall we bear it all?
    How many more red years?
Story it and glory it and share it all,
    In seas of blood and tears?
They are braggart attitudes we've worn so long;
They are tinsel platitudes we've sworn so long—
    We who have turned the Devil's Grindstone,
        Borne with the hell called War!

The Dundee Advertiser, 3 January 1915

J B Nicholson

ON HEARING A LARK SINGING AT DAWN IN THE TRENCHES

O Wonder Bird, what song is this you sing?
   What message to us weary, war-worn men?
Is it to memories of peace you cling?
   Of sunlit strath and flower-bejewelled glen?

Would you remind us of quiet country lanes?
   Of ivied homesteads nestling among the hills?
Of rose-cheeked maids meandering with their swains?
   Of pebbly rivulets and whispering rills?

Or do your notes protest against the fate
   That forced you, neutral, from your love-lined nest
To share the humans' agony of hate
   That found no echo in your joyous breast?

I think at times you mock great man's strange mind,
   Which, civilised, creates an Earthly Hell,
Calling it war; red murder of a kind
   Undreamt by Attila before he fell.

There was a tremble in your song just now
   That spoke of mate, of child-birds lost to you.
O Wonder Bird, we watchers marvel how,
   Your wings still flutter in that sky of blue.

Haste, herald lark, for soon your sister tune
   Will die amid the discord of the guns;
The heavens will shriek in agony by noon.
   Hide, Wonder Bird . . .

The Dundee Advertiser, 3 June 1915

J B Nicholson

THE CRUCIFIX

He hung there at the crossroads
On a Cross of rain-beat red,
And the nails that pierced His hands and feet
And the thorn-crown on His head
Showed awfully in the moonlight,
And it seemed that He was dead.

But I knelt beneath the Crucifix
And prayed with bowèd head,
And the nails that pierced His hands and feet
Fell out, all rusted red,
And shining in the moonlight
Was a gold crown on His head.

And He came from off the Crucifix,
He who had seemed dead,
And gently placed His piercèd hand
In mine; and so He led
Me in the paling moonlight
To a place all bloody red.

'Here was a soldier's sacrifice',
He gently to me said.
'Here a man fell as was his meet,
For justice; and he bled
There in the ghostly moonlight
Till they said that he was dead.

But I saw him from yon Crucifix,
And I came with noiseless tread,
And took his heart and placed it
In a babe unborn instead,
And his soul sped in the moon light,
And with God's in Heaven was wed.

And the babe shall be a hero,
Of that soldier's valour bred.
He shall live to lead his brothers,
But not in battle red:
He shall lead them to the sunlight,
When the Hell of War is dead'.

I awoke there at the crossroads
By the cross of rain-beat red.
     *   *   *

And the nails that pierced His hands and feet
And the thorn-crown on His head
Showed awfully in the moonlight.
     *   *   *

But I knew He was not dead.

The Dundee Advertiser, 5 June 1915

David M Nicoll

A MOONLIGHT REVERIE

Night o'er the earth its sombre curtain draws,
Precludes the light and muffles all in gloom;
Phoebus his enlivening smile withdraws,
And Phoebe, queen of the stilly night,
  Reigns in his room.
Clad in a lustrous robe of shimmering white
  Her throne she mounts
And by the radiant light of her own sweet face
  Makes glad the gloom.
This same sad moon, now rolling high,
Lights up a world embrued in bloody war,
And countless thousands stark and stiff,
Lie with upturned faces to the moonlit sky;
Brave hearts! they gave their life in freedom's cause
To check the cruel oppressor's lustful pride;
Belgians and British, Russians and French,
In heroes' graves lie sleeping side by side.
Perchance, All-Seeing One on high
Looks down with pitying eye on this,
And the recording angel writes their names,
And opes for them the gates of Paradise.

The Dundee Advertiser, 29 May 1915

Frederick Niven

TO LANCE-CORPORAL JOSEPH LEE
(Black Watch—Somewhere in France)

Fain would I too, for Liberty,
    Dare Death; yet here I must remain
Till Beauty seemeth sad to me
    And discord mars each sweet refrain.

This year I cannot take delight
    In England's manifold display—
In apple-blossom, snowy white,
    In yellow lilac, purple may.

Because this arabesque of sun
    And leaf-shade in the airy wood,
You loved as well as anyone,
    You of the scholar-gipsy mood;

And I am here—and you are there,
    So I have anguish 'mid these trees;
This (like so much) doth seem unfair—
    That you should fight while I have ease.

Yet, Joseph, as my case is rent
    With anguish here, may you, in France,
'Mid warfare taste some high content,
    Hear music 'mid the dissonance.

The Dundee Advertiser, 12 June 1915

Non Sibi Sed Patriae

CALVARY IN FRANCE

Why should I mourn to Thee, Thou Father-God,
  Who gav'st Thy Son to die for all the world?
Thou gav'st to me a son, and him I bore
  And lov'd, nor dreamt he'd see war-flags unfurl'd.

He was a man-child, and he heard the call
  That drew the nations to the field in strife,
Yet, mother-wise, I saw with mother's eyes
  And pitied him, and loved, and craved him life.

But he has died—a sacrifice for what
  Is world-old, as power of kings, who prance
Hell-shod o'er nations. He has been a lesser Christ
  Who died upon a later Calvary in France.

The tears have made my old eyes red, but now
  The bitterness of sorrow past, I mourn no more.
He won to glory in his death, for he has died
  That good may come. Yet, Lord, my heart is sore.

The Dundee Advertiser, 12 November 1915

Max Philpot

TO CORPORAL ANGUS, VC

When the foot of the Teuton touched Belgian soil,
    And Britain's fair honour was tried,
When up through the gloom rose the names of our Great,
    Who for Justice and Honour had died,

When the taunt of the tyrant shed Malice's veil,
    The taunt that our army was small,
When the menacing legions of arrogant Force
    Determined on Liberty's fall:

From mine and mill, from castle and cot,
    Came the chivalrous sons of our race,
And you, Willie Angus—the pride of our Shire—
    Took a front and resolute place.

And true to the traits our traditions unfold,
    Of Daring and Love inter-grown;
You rescued a life from the hazard of death
    By quite forgetting your own.

We hail thee as Hero, we treasure thy deed—
    A deed now accepted by Fame—
And Glory declares an immortal response
    To brave Willie Angus's name.

The Dundee Advertiser, 6 September 1915

Max Philpot

MULTAM IN PARVO

For days and weeks they waited
For word from Jim, for word from Jim;
And though they felt, they never stated—
'It's not like him, it's not like him'.

They prayed and hoped and doubted—
Yes, Faith did wane, yes, Faith did wane,
For fears could not be routed:
They prayed again, they prayed again.

Dark grew the world around them—
Dark as the grave, dark as the grave;
Old age at last had found them,
And nought could save, and nought could save.

But—one night a letter fell
Behind the door, behind the door,
It came from C——, Jim was well:
They're young once more, they're young once more.

The Dundee Advertiser, 9 September 1915

Lance-Corporal Pit

THE THIN RED LINE

We don't intend to talk about the things that we can do;
We're only Kitchener's Army, but our hearts are brave and true;
So we won't disgrace the honour that was won in years lang syne,
By the Boys at Balaclava in the thin Red LIne.

Chorus

You may talk about your Gordons and your Gallant Forty-Twa,
Your silver streakit Seaforths, and your Camerons so Braw,
But gi'e to me the tartan o' the lads that look so fine
Wi' the wavin' six and bonnie dice, the Thin Red Line.

You may talk about your officers—well we ha'e got a few!
There's MacNeil our gallant Colonel, and Johnnie Campbell, too;
When they start to worry William, he will very soon opine
They're the pertinacious bulldogs of the Thin Red Line.

When we went to war in Germany the Kaiser told us a'
That an army so contemptible was hardly worth a straw.
He said he'd sweep us all away, wi' bluster asinine,
But his broom was badly broken by the flint rock line.

Our gallant little army was outnumbered ten to one,
And couldn't take advantage of the noble deeds they'd done;
So the call came from Lord Kitchener that we should all combine
To fight for King and country in the khaki line.

Now, to gang and be a sodger—o' that we never thocht,
We were simple working laddies, contented where we wrocht;
But we wouldna wear white feathers, so we hurried out to jine,
And went to help our brothers in the Thin Red Line.

Since that time we've been through it, boys, in barracks and
                                             in camp,
Drilling and manoeuvring, wi' many a mile to tramp;
And often, though we stuck it, we've been tempted to repine,
And wish we'd never listed in the Thin Red Line.

100

But, cheer up, lads, the time is comin' when ye'll get the chance
Of showin' what you're made of, in the great advance;
And may the sun of vict'ry on the Allied Armies shine,
And the first to enter Berlin be the Thin Red Line.

The People's Journal, 22 May 1915

Isabella Jane Reid

A WOMAN'S PLEA
(Shade of Kingsley—Pardon)

Be brave sweetheart, and let who will be clever;
　Live noble deeds, not read them all day long;
'Tis ours to break the power of traitrous foemen
　Not serenade fair beauty with a song.

Good charity hath cloak both wide and ample
　But hide not thou, sweetheart, beneath its fold.
Leave that refuge free for babes and women,
　Know thou that Truth for Falsehood hath been sold.

Let other folk give raiment to the needy,
　Do thou such tasks to older men assign;
But go thou forth, thy manhood strong and fearless,
　To where thy brothers sleep near flowing Rhine.

Their blood cries out from earth, not brown but crimson;
　'Twould call thee quickly to the gory fray
Whilst fighting thou shalt hear the spirit legions
　Bidding thee follow on the victor's way.

What if the shell of foeman should slay thee—
　Count thou the honour greater than thy life
'Tis not death to fall in Freedom's battle;
　Dead is that man who stays him from the strife.

The Dundee Advertiser, 24 May 1915

102

J R Russell

TO THE BLACK WATCH AT THE FRONT

A message frae the hameland,
   A greeting to ye a',
Brave soldiers of our own Black Watch,
   The gallant Forty Twa.

With proud but anxious hearts we read
   How in the battle stern
The Highlander in art of war
   Has nothing new to learn.

For hovering o'er these faithful fields,
   The spirit of your sires,
Who fought and won in days of old,
   To valiant deeds inspires.

The rivers of your mountain land
   In winter spate are rushing,
So your wild charge drives through the foe,
   All fierce resistance crushing.

Frae mony a maid's and mother's heart
   In Tayside and Dundee,
The prayer ascends and echoes round
   The Kingdom by the sea,

That He who rules the world in right
   May with his sheltering arm
Protect and guard the lads they love,
   And keep them frae all harm.

The Dundee Advertiser, 26 January 1915

G M S

MOTHERS

Oh, Mothers! The Empire needeth
The sons ye bravely bore.
Oh, Mothers! The Empire calleth
   Your sons to end the War.

Will ye hesitate, oh Mothers,
In your Country's agony,
To send your sons, with willing hearts,
   To set Great Britain free?

What though the heart grows heavy,
Oh, Mothers, tired the hand—
Think of the glorious offering,
   Ye Mothers give the land.

And if Fate wills that, Mothers,
Your sons fall fighting there,
Say, though your hearts be breaking,
   'Thank God, he did his share'.

The Dundee Advertiser, 7 October 1915

R A S

SHOT AT HIS POST

'Mid the rush, the roar, the rattle,
'Mid the blood and blaze of battle,
While batter'd trenches burst with leaden hail,
   Might the horrors of such night
   Dull the soul and dim the sight?
Might the fire of youthful courage flicker—fail?

'Shot at his post in the morning mist—'
   This was the message from over the foam,
And the letters were fondly, tenderly kiss'd
   By the trembling lips of a mother at home.
She heard in a dream the roar of the guns
   And the crash of the bursting shell,
And she saw the flame in his eyes—her son's—
   As facing the foeman he fell.
   'Shot at his post—'
   Her lov'd and her lost
'Twas an end to her hopes and her fears;
   And weeping she cried,
   'For his country he died'.
And smiling she dried her tears.

'Shot at his post in the morning mist—'
   Oh, break not the bleeding and bruisèd heart!
No glorious death on Honour's list
   Was his, who played no hero's part.
Ah! dazed he stood as the shots rang out
   From a file of his comrade's guns,
And the grass was red with the crimson gout
   That gashed from his bosom—her son's.
   'Shot at his post—'
   Dishonoured and lost,
Yet she dreams of her soldier brave!
   But the hearts of men
   Are in heaven's own ken,
And its tears may bejewel his grave.

The Dundee Advertiser, 28 April 1915

James S Scotland

IN MEMORIAM
(Mr J Beveridge Nicholson)

While mourning deeply our departed friend,
Let us not speak of an untimely end.
Have we not faith in God, or has it fled
Since he was numbered with the silent dead.

The case is not the jewel it contains;
The case is gone, but still the pearl remains.
His body rests beneath a foreign sod,
But white-robed angels bore his soul to God.

His course, now finished here, is but begun
In that fair land that needs nor Moon nor Sun,
A land of righteousness and peace and joy,
Where sorrow never comes nor pleasures cloy;
That knows no raging storms, no dreadful night,
But love eternal sheds eternal Light.

The Dundee Advertiser, 23 July 1915

F Shepherd

A CALL TO ARMS

Wake up! ye sons of Scotland,
   And answer to the call,
And help to win her battles.
   Would you see your country fall?
Would you like to see her trampled
   By the proud contemptuous foe?
Up, up, my boys, and at them,
   And lay the tyrants low.

Already men are joining
   The colours, far and near,
And leaving wives and children
   And homes that they hold dear.
Already strife is stirring
   Not very far away;
The fiery cross is going
   Through the Highlands
      Day by day.

So, up, my boys, and answer
   Your country's glorious call;
For love of home and country,
   I know you'd give your all.

The People's Journal, 2 January 1915

G Speed

THE GALLANT FOURTH
A Signaller's Tribute to His Dashing Fellows

The sound of the guns fills the air with its thunder,
    The bullets in showers fall faster than rain;
There are gaps in the ranks, men are torn asunder
    But the time is not ripe for the attack to begin.

The regiment of highlanders, impatient and eager,
    Crouch in a trench for the word to advance.
The cannon fire slackens, the word is 'Get ready';
    We'll strike a great blow for old Scotland and France.

Forward the Fourth, your duty's before you;
    Yours is the honour to win or to die.
Shrapnel was bursting, machine guns were rattling,
    Comrades were falling, yet 'On' was the cry.

Into that hell, where the lurking foe waited,
    Safe behind barriers, mowing them down,
As if on parade, went the gallant regiment
    Forward to death or undying renown.

They gain the position, the foe flees before them,
    The order is given to halt and to rest.
Theirs to obey, though at heart they are eager
    To meet with the foe and prove which is the best.

The German positions that day were all taken,
    The whole British Army proved what they were worth;
And we'll rank with the bravest that brave Highland
                      regiment,
    Dundee's own Battalion, the gallant old Fourth.

Then long may they stand for their country's glory
    We pray, God of Battles, their guiding star be;
Give them victories to come in the battles before them,
    And bring them safe home to 'Bonnie Dundee'.

The People's Journal, 22 May 1915

L M Stewart

THE BULLET'S LITTLE BIT

They harrowed me out of my native ground,
    Where I lay in the quartz and clay;
They broke the rocks that had hemmed me round
    As demons that hold to their prey.
With rubble and stone and grit and scree
    They barrowed me through their mines;
Then raised me to the burnished lea,
And this was all they said of me—
    'The grey lead never shines'.

I looked at them through their furnace bars
    Whilst the flame-tongues they leapt at me,
And brown slag hung like the battle-scars
    Of corpses that float on the sea.
I thought as the sweat poured down like rain
    Such men might be brave and true:
This golden thought ran through my brain—
'The lead hath victories to gain,
    The lead hath work to do'.

A bullet, they sent me with shot and shell,
    Where we ravaged the rampant Hun;
A marksman got me at Neuve Chapelle,
    And blasted me out of a gun.
Right down to the enemy-lines I tore,
    A Brandenburg rogue got hit;
The rascal fell, then coughed and swore,
Whilst round him trickled streams of gore:
    'The lead had done its bit!'

The Dundee Advertiser, 5 July 1915

L M Stewart

A DIRGE
(In Memory of the Late Bertrand Stewart)

Achara is weary and Appin is lone,
Her clansmen have raised him a tablet of stone,
A knight of the race far away on the Aisne
Sleeps softly at rest in the village of Braisne.

A cross at his head, and sweet honour his mail;
So make me lament for a son of the Gael;
Let moorland and mountain—our old Highland lair—
Ring loudly again by the Castle Stalcaire.

The wail of the pibroch shall course like the haär,
When winter drives over the red fields of war;
The coronach-note let us spread like the hail
O'er the sheilings of Appin, the land of the Gael.

Blithe Appin maids, weep ye, and cry ye ochone,
A Stewart has fallen: he falls not alone.
The tombs of your lovers are scattered like grain,
Far off in the land of the village of Braisne.

Weep, women of Appin, weep loudly and wail;
The tartan lies red in the blood of the Gael;
A knight of the race, far away on the Aisne,
Sleeps softly at rest in the village of Braisne.

The Dundee Advertiser, 10 August 1915

110

L M Stewart

SEPTEMBER AND PEACE

Hail, sweet September, chaste and full of peace:
Brimful and rich, and blest with nature's store:
Behold again the travail of a nation's ease,
And on a country's sorrows and her suff'rings pour
The healing and anointing oil of Peace.
Yea, Peace, but yet no craven Peace bestow
On those who battle in the nation's cause;
Unfetter thou the war-worn soldier's brow
And give him the abiding peace that comes
To him who stands rockfast and shields the laws
And guards his country's altars and its homes,
As true hearts beat unto a nation's melodies,
Drop thou upon the distant mound a harvest tear:
While sad winds chant o'er hill and vale their threnodies,
Rain gold and gossamer upon the soldier's bier.

    *   *   *

When life's wan shreds and her frail strands seem worn and
                 done,
Weave laurel leaf and myrtle in the worker's crest,
For lo, the shocks of earth will russet on the sun
While his lone heart is coming to an everlasting rest.

The Dundee Advertiser, 3 September 1915

L M Stewart

ALONE

Yonder stands the ploughman's cot,
Dank by the western foam,
And oft that ploughman turned the sod
There, by his island home.

Once he loved a mountain lass:
Now his last tryst is o'er;
The country's flag surrounds his bones:
His grave a foreign shore.

Loud beats the surf: beside that cot
A frail heart sobs unknown:
The grey gull shrieks a rabid note:
The ploughman's ears are stone.

The Dundee Advertiser, 20 September 1915

L M Stewart

THE WALTZING HOOF

While o'er the massive plains of war
  The lagging clouds depend,
Still deeper from the throat of heaven
  The winter snows descend.

And ever as the hot shells kiss
  The pallid belts of snow,
The horsemen cry, the steel blades flash,
  Battalions come and go.

And ever as the fight rolls on
  The sabres turn to red,
As o'er the sod in thousands lie
  The wounded and the dead.

Beside the graves, beside the lea,
  Beside the copsewood and the fells,
Where'er the squadrons gather now
  Is passing on the chime of bells.

Far off, far off, where bugles blow,
  The wildered notes of beauty flow;
The tinkle as of elfin bells—
  The horsemen waltzing through the snow.

And as the dying fall to rest
  Far off in the rear of human woe,
A call is there of yuletide bells—
  The horseman riding through the snow.

The Dundee Advertiser, 25 November 1915

Maggie Todd

PEACE VERSUS WAR

Of war as something to be sung,
   An open door to feats of arms,
You think—ah! friend, but you are young—
   And peace for age hath wondrous charms.

'But peace', you say, 'is bought with blood',
   To which I humbly make reply,
'Less deep would flow the crimson flood
   Did not ambition soar so high!'

'Ah! but ambition must be met
   And combated', I hear you say;
'It would not do for us to let
   Ambition over us have sway'.

Yet, prithee, do not take amiss,
   If thinking on those fields afar,
I say my warmest prayer is this—
   'God, end this cruel, cruel war'.

By war's accumulated woe,
   I still must think the better plan
For weary mortals here below
   To live at peace with God and man.

And yet our praise shall never cease
   Of soldier brave and gallant tar,
Who, just that we may live in peace
   Have entered now the ranks of war.

The Dundee Advertiser, 23 January 1915

Maggie Todd

THE CALL TO ARMS

'The tide has turned in Flanders,
They will not need you now';
But aye I saw the shadow
Of gloom upon his brow.

'The tide has turned in Flanders,
No thanks to me,' he said;
'In that stupendous struggle
No blood of mine was shed.

'I saw the path before me,
I shunned it for your sake;
Aye, shunned the path which others
The courage had to take.

'Tho' sore on my soul's honour,
I feel the stain today—
And it's oh! to be in Flanders
To wipe that stain away!'

Such was my son's ambition
I honoured him for it;
He goes with my permission
To do 'his little bit'.

To lend his little effort,
To break the cruel foe—
Who would not be in Flanders
With will and strength to go?

The Dundee Advertiser, 13 May 1915

Touchstone

MACHINE GUNS

I can talk as fast as five-and-twenty file,
  Despite my quaint and captivating stutter;
I can check a German mass attack in style
  With the thousand little telling things I utter.
I'm a tricky little party, I admit,
  And my mechanism takes a bit of knowing;
Though I wouldn't tell a cram, and I have been known to jam,
  You should hear me when I once get fairly going!

The Bosches early tumbled to my worth
  In keeping all intruders at a distance;
When their legions started out to claim the earth
  They were keen upon obtaining my assistance.
The British thought me useful in the night,
  Or a handy little adjunct in surprises,
But today the fact is known I can more than hold my own
  On any old occasion that arises.

The Dundee Advertiser, 31 August 1915

William G Whyte

LAMENT OF A SCOTS GREY HORSE

Oh, waes me, but my he'rt is sair, tho' but a horse am I,
My Scottish pride is wounded and amang the dust mawn lie;
I used to be a braw Scots Grey, but noo I'm khaki clad,
My auld grey coat has disappeared, the thocht o't makes me sad.

My Scots Grey coat was aye my pride, sae glossy an sae braw
An' everywhere I went it was admired by ane an' a';
I'm yellow noo frae head tae tail, it pains my he'rt sae true,
Oh, bonnie Scotland, what I'm suffering for ye noo.

My jacket's like my master's noo; he laughed in fiendish glee,
As he plied his brush an' aye stood back tae hae a look at me.
'Oh, Jim,' I cried, 'hae mercy mon, my grey coat I adore;
Hoo will they ken that I'm a Scot—a Scots Horse to the core'.

But Jim my master, painted on, his face wreathed in a smile,
He slapped the paint on me an' sang, 'The Lass o' Ballochmyle',
An' when tae my rear he went wi' his hateful brush an' pail,
Oh, just tae melt his Scottish he'rt I wagged my auld grey tail.

Alas, alas, my auld grey tail, he even painted that;
It was my pride while at the front, though it's aye at my back;
An' when the wet paint stained my tail, the saut tears dimmed
                                                    my e'e,
Oh, I'll never wag my tail again until the day I dee.

Oh, what's a coat o' khaki broon compared with Scottish grey?
It canna mak' me braver in the hot and bloody fray;
Proud, proud was I to be a Grey, but, ah, they've painted me,
An' now I'm like a donkey mair than half on the spree.

It mak's me think o' bygone days, when I roamed in yon vale,
An' whisked the flies frae aff my back sae proudly wi' my tail,
Then cantered up the steep brae side, an' galloped ower the lea,
The proudest grey in Scotland—bonnie Scotland over the sea.

But changed, alas, noo is the scene; on a sunny Belgian plain
I carry yin o' Scotland's sons o'er fields o' pride an' pain,
An' faithfully I'll carry him within the bloody fray,
Altho' he made me khaki broon an' scorned my Scottish grey.

I ken it's a' for freedom's sake that I am here this day,
Sae faur awa' frae Scotland an' my native howe an' brae,
An' tho' I'm but a humble horse, I'll suffer wi' the lave,
To free us frae the German yoke or find a Belgian grave.

So Jim, dear master, should ye fa', a bullet in your breast,
An' on the plains of Belgium find a Scottish soldier's rest,
I'll stand across your body, Jim, an' guard ye till I dee,
An' may the Lord forgi'e ye for the way you painted me.

The Dundee Advertiser, 4 January 1915

M'Landburgh Wilson

MORTAL WOUNDS

He who follows fife and drum
When he hears the bullets hum
Knows that death but once may come;
   Red and salt
     Swells the flood,
  Blood and tears,
    Tears and blood.

She who waits to weep her slain
Finds no easing of the pain,
Finds that death's not quenched by rain;
   Salt and red
     Grow the spears,
  Tears and blood,
    Blood and tears.

The Dundee Advertiser, 20 April 1915

NOTES

p 3   There were many requests in the papers for presents for those at the Front. Thanks were often sent home in verse form. See pp 18 and 38.

p 5   This poem is an imitation of *The Lay of the Last Minstrel*, 6.1. It was written in response to Mr Asquith's speech at Newcastle about it being 'the nation's war': '. . . this is the nation's war, and no man among us in the vast audience, or among the millions of our fellow-countrymen outside . . . is worthy of the name of British citizen who is not taking his part in it.'

p 6   'Eye-Witness': this is a reference to 'Eye-Witness's Diary', the regular report from the Front sent to the newspapers by an 'Eye-Witness' present at General Headquarters.

p 10   This poem was sent to the paper by Corporal W M Robb of the 44th Field Bakery who said it had been written by a friend; it may well have been by Robb himself.

p 17   'The Piper of Loos' of this poem was Piper Laidlaw of the 7th Battalion, the King's Own Scottish Borderers; he was awarded the VC for playing his pipes under fire and whilst seriously wounded at the Battle of Loos, in order to encourage the men. There were several heroic stories of pipers at Loos; Piper David Simpson, 2nd Battalion the Black Watch, who came from Buckhaven, was another piper whose story was acclaimed; he was killed at Loos whilst playing the Black Watch battle tune as the men advanced towards the German line.

p 19   The Battle of Neuve Chapelle began on 10 March 1915.

p 25   The first known treaty between Scotland and France was the Franco-Scottish Alliance ('the Auld Alliance') of 1295.

p 27   See 'The Green Grass', p 71.

p 34   Armstrong Barry was a Dundee solicitor; during the war he helped to form a voluntary committee to assist the widows and dependents of serving men and he became Honorary Secretary of the society then formed, the City of Dundee Branch of the Incorporated Soldiers' and Sailors' Help Society. He published a volume of war and other poems, *Laurel and Myrtle* (1918).

p 36   On his return from the Front, just before this poem was written, Mr John Redmond commented: 'To go down the centre of the street you have to climb over . . . broken statues of the Virgin.'

p 38   J R Black was in the London Scottish Regiment; these verses were written in acknowledgement of gifts from Leslie Parish Church Bible Class.

p 39   Sergeant F M Cockburn was in the Nilgrin Volunteer Rifles, India.

p 40   C N Craig was a Sergeant in the Machine Gun Section of the 4th Black Watch; he fought at Neuve Chapelle and at Loos, where he was working the machine guns on the right flank of the attack.

p 48   Bandmaster Etherington was in the 2/5th Battalion, Royal Scots Fusiliers.
Bugler Patrick Golden, who came from Castle Street, Broughty Ferry, was a 15 year-old boy-soldier in the RSF Band; he joined the 1/5th RSF, in March 1915 and was sent to the Dardanelles. There he was recommended for the DCM after going out under fire in front of the trenches to rescue a wounded bugler; then, despite receiving several bullet wounds, he went out a second time to rescue another wounded man. Golden's father served in the Black Watch for twelve years and was, during the war, a drill instructor at Rumbling Bridge.

p 52   See Joseph Lee's poems pp 69–77. 'Wonder-bird' appears to be a reference to the death of J B Nicholson on 13 July 1915; this poem seems to suggest that Nicholson's poetic gift has been passed into the care of Lee. See Nicholson's poem, p 92.
    'When "Mac" prepared his palace grand': a reference to a poem by Lee, 'Macfarlane's Dug-out'.

p 58   'Bound in life's bundle with my Lord to lie': see I Samuel 25:29.

p 60   'One Shall Be Taken': see St Matthew 24:40; 'Death . . . victory': see I Corinthians 15:55

p 63   J W Jack came from Glenfarg; he often had poems in French published in *The Dundee Advertiser*.

p 64   See Joseph Lee's poems pp 69–77.

p 67   The Reverend Joseph Leckie, DD, was Minister of the Boston United Free Church, Cupar.

p 69   Joseph Lee was a member of the editorial staff of *The People's Journal*. Already well-known in Dundee before the war as a journalist, poet, artist and cartoonist, he enlisted in the 4th Black Watch and was sent to France early in 1915. Though he quickly rose to the rank of Sergeant, he at first refused to take a commission; he was finally commissioned Lieutenant in the King's Royal Rifle Corps in 1917 and on his return to the Western Front he was captured by the Germans; he spent the rest of the war in a Prisoner of War camp at Carlsruhe. The poems in this book are a small selection of the many poems he sent home for publication in the local newspapers; they were later published in the two volumes *Ballads of Battle* (1916) and *Work-a-Day Warriors* (1917). Lee died on 17 May 1949.

p 75   'Linton' was   Lance-Corporal Linton Andrews (later Sir Linton Andrews) who, before the war, had been a member of the editorial staff of *The Dundee Advertiser*. Together with a number of his press colleagues he joined the 4th Black Watch early in the war. He spent three years at the Western Front and after the war he wrote *The Haunting Years* about his experiences there. He later became editor of *The Yorkshire Post* and Chairman of the Press Council; he died in 1972 at the age of eighty-six.

'Jack' was J B Nicholson who was killed on 13 July 1915; See Nicholson's poems pp 92–94.

p 76   'La Croix Rouge': a reference to the great crucifix of a grey figure on a wooden cross painted red, in the French village of Rouge Croix; it was a landmark well-known to the men of the 4th Black Watch.

p 78   See Joseph Lee's poems pp 69–77.

p 81   The Germans captured La Bassée in 1914 and despite many British counter-attacks they held it throughout the war.

p 83   Piper J M'Lellan, DCM, was in the Argyll and Sutherland Highlanders.

p 85   'Nap': in the card-game of that name 'nap' is the call of five which is a 'risk-all-win-all' situation.

'Euchre': card-game in which advantage is gained over an opponent by his failure to take three tricks.

p 86   W D M came from Dundee.

This poem imitates the rhythmic patterns and rhyme scheme of Robert Burns's 'Scots, Wha Hae'.

Men of the 4th Black Watch were reputed to have shouted 'Marmalade' and 'On the ba'' when they went 'over the top' on the morning of 25 September 1915, the first day of the Battle of Loos. This story was widely reported in the papers of the time. The connection between Dundee and Keiller's marmalade (one of the three Js) was well-known.

p 87   'Mater Militis': i.e. soldier's mother . . .

p 92   J B Nicholson: John Beveridge Nicholson was a member of the staff of *The People's Journal*. Son of the Reverend T B Nicholson of the United Free Church in Dunfermline, he joined the 4th Black Watch at the outbreak of war and went with them to France early in 1915. He was killed by a sniper's bullet on 13 July 1915 and is buried in the military cemetery of Richebourt St Vaast.

p 93   'The Crucifix': refers to La Croix Rouge; see note to p 76 above.

p 96   See Joseph Lee's poems pp 69–77.

p 97   'Non sibi sed Patriae': i.e. not for him himself but for our country.

p 98   Max Philpot was a prolific writer of poems to the local papers; many of them were published in his volume *Many Moods* (1917). Corporal William

Angus of the 8th Highland Light Infantry came from Carluke; he was awarded the VC for rescuing one of his officers, Lieutenant Martin, under heavy fire. Angus was known as a reluctant hero who did not want to be the centre of attention.

'taunt that our army was small': *The Times* for 1 October 1914 reported that in an order from his headquarters Kaiser Wilhelm described the British Expeditionary Force as 'General French's contemptible little army'.

p 99   'Multam in parvo': i.e. Much in little.

p 100   The 'thin red line' refers to the 93rd Sutherland Highlanders who, wearing their scarlet tunics, repelled the Russian attack on Balaclava in 1854.

'Gallant Forty-Twa': the phrase originates from the exploits of Sergeant Samuel McGaw, VC, of the Black Watch at the Battle of Amoafu (West Africa) in 1874.

'an army so contemptible': see note to p 98 above.

p 102   This poem is based on Charles Kingsley's 'A Farewell to C E G', which begins with the well-known line, 'Be good, sweet maid, and let who can be clever'.

p 103   'The gallant Forty Twa': see note to p 100 above.

p 105   R A S came from Brechin.

p 106   'Mr J Beveridge Nicholson': see note to p 92 above.

p 108   Signaller George Speed (1894–1968), who had earlier worked for John Leng and Company, enlisted in the 4th Black Watch at the outbreak of war and went with them to France; he fought in the Battle of Neuve Chapelle, to which this poem, written at the Front, refers, and afterwards at Loos. He later received a commission and became a Lieutenant in the Royal Scots Fusiliers; he was wounded at Passchendaele.

p 109   'bit': presumably a reference to the recruiting poster asking men to 'do [their] bit for King and Country'.

p 114   Maggie Todd was born in 1862 in Camperdown, Dundee. Her father was a miller and in 1878 the family moved to Windy Mill, Murroes. Maggie was a regular contributor of poems to *The People's Journal* and *The Weekly News*; she won the *Journal's* Queen's Diamond Jubilee competition for poetry. In 1900 she published a book of poems *Burnside Lyrics*. The latter part of her life was spent in Kellas where she died in 1958, aged ninety-four.

p 115   'his little bit': see note to p 109 above.

117   William Whyte came from Linlithgow.
This poem refers to an order that grey horses should be painted khaki, since their grey coats showed up too much and made them a target for enemy fire.

Have you forgotten yet? . . .
Look up, and swear by the green of the spring that
you'll never forget.

Siegfried Sassoon

Dundee Second World War Memorial: 1939–1945 'To the Memory of All
Ranks of the 4th and 5th Dundee and Angus Battalions of the Black Watch
who died in the Second World War'.